Broken Arrow: A Nuke Goes Missing

Copyright © 2019 by Manfred Leuthard

Revision 2, minor corrections, 02/17/2022

Published by Manfred Leuthard through Kindle Publishing

Title page Font made from Online Web Fonts is licensed by CC(Creative Commons) by 3.0

Print Font is Palatino

Cover design by John Lutheran

Edited by Catherine Parnell

Requests for review copies: manfred@manfredleuthard.com

First Printing, 2020, printed in USA

Paperback ISBN	978-1-7349135-0-7
Hardcover ISBN	978-1-7349135-1-4
Apple/Kindle ISBN	978-1-7349135-2-1

Broken Arrow: A Nuke goes Missing

A Thriller

Manfred Leuthard

Prologue

My name is Harry Scott Anderson. I am fifty-two years old. I live and work in Santa Fe, New Mexico. I fly helicopters for anyone that can afford such an exclusive way to travel. I enjoy what I do a great deal, since it beats working for a living. For fun I cook, read, and engage in the never-ending pursuit of female companionship. This is the story of my adventures in 2015.

Where's the Dog?

May 2015, Jemez Mountains, New Mexico

Christine Salazar is in a great mood; it's the end of a busy work week, the weather is getting warmer by the day, and she is looking forward to a pleasant, lazy weekend. A low, thin overcast is drifting in from the west. It is late in the day, almost dinnertime, and the bold colors seen on *National Geographic* screen savers are gradually migrating towards the anemic greys of a Cinema Noir poster. She is blissfully unaware of what awaits her.

She decides to make a short detour on her way home from a staff meeting at the Bandelier administrative facilities. She prefers to be called Chris, and that short form, often reserved for males, is compatible with her appearance and the aura of self-confidence that she radiates. The drive from the park to her home in Nambe takes about forty minutes; therefore, a short detour will still get her home in time for dinner. This evening she drives her personal car. She is a freelancer, working for state and federal government agencies on the lethally boring topic of Interagency Data Exchange, a feeble attempt to quiet the turf war between agencies whose overlapping responsibilities, both geographic and functional, puts them in perpetual conflict. Frustrating work that pays well. Work that frees up a lot of time to pursue other goals. Goals like writing the "Mother of all who-done-it novels." She's made it to page forty by now.

The Juniper Campground near White Rock and Los Alamos justifies its existence by its proximity to Bandelier National Monument. A vast plateau is flanked by deep ravines, many ending at the Rio Grande below. Lots of Ponderosa pines, clusters of aspens. Not enough water for cottonwoods. Whole sections of what once was a dense forest are now devoid of all branches and leaves, blackened by fire, pointing skywards like oversized chopsticks. Some meadows that resulted from the wildfires are sprouting new aspens.

The campground is situated at about seven thousand feet elevation, near the monument's entrance. Occasional harsh winters at that elevation impose limits; it is operational, although unattended, from spring till fall. Near the first couple of camping spots, the weary traveler will find a roof-covered notice board, lots of info there, and all that is needed for a self-service style check-in and check-out. Bandelier is of interest to those holding a fascination with ancient Native American tribes, extinct cliff dwelling societies, or hikers who love the trails through the cool Jemez mountains. Other than on some holidays, mostly at the beginning and the end of the tourist season, it never fills up. The Park Service formally is charged with operating the campground, but in reality, pays not much attention. An occasional complaint about loud parties or trash left behind by an inconsiderate camper will trigger a brief visit by a park ranger, most often to simply chastise the offenders. Such an intervention is generally followed by a slow cruise over the short couple loops that service the campsites – a meek display of adult supervision. The problem repertoire consists of no more significant threats than barking dogs, misbehaving children, and the occasional juvenile drug experiment. The Colorado border is only ninety minutes away, and with it is near-legal pot.

Chris's detour leads to the farthest corner of the campground. She was "volunteered" to set up a car rally at an event tailored to bring staff together. One of those you-must-attend-it-will-be-loads-of-fun events.

A decade working for the Las Cruces Police Department, rising to the lofty, nay the esteemed level of Lead Detective, changed her. Changed her both for better and for worse: she developed into a sharp, observant, and competent detective while losing all remnants of ambition for the next level potentially available through promotion. As a female police officer with a Hispanic last name, one justified "use of lethal force" incident notched on her belt, in a small town on the Mexican border, she had reached her Glass Ceiling. Office politics, in general, and kissing ass specifically, is held in low esteem by Chris. She had given serious consideration to "sleeping her way to the top." Still, after counting the number of superiors, both male and some female in her path, she decided that this approach was fraught with peril and did not seriously pursue it. Not seriously. She somehow managed to be seen by her male colleagues and bosses as probably lesbian, and by the females in her social and professional environment as undecided. These hasty judgments were primarily based on her unfortunate tendency to shop for her clothes at REI, regardless of the occasion she was buying for. This ambiguity left a lot of people confused, and it kept her separated from any resemblance of a balanced social life. Period.

Nowadays, she's a volunteer with the Santa Fe County Sheriff's department who, other than the tribal cop from Pojoaque, covers the law enforcement needs of the Nambe village and Pueblo. And the tribal cop is not well-liked among anyone not of Native American heritage. The distaste finds its origin due to the tribal cop having the habit of writing DWC tickets – Driving While Caucasian.

Chris pulls into the campground turnoff, lowers the driver side window, drops the speed first to ten, then five, and as she goes around the first left turn, is about to pass a lovely, large motor home towing a small SUV, with warm air still dancing out of the RV's engine compartment in the rear, the SUV still attached with a tow bar. The two vehicles must have recently arrived. The license plate in the back shows that the vehicle is registered in Missouri, the implication being that these visitors are likely unfamiliar with the area. Next to the stairs to the entry door, a sealed, large sack of dog food rests against the tire. Purina, all-organic, non-GMO dog food for the athletic, adult, large breed, the packaging states. Classy. So, where is the Evian for the dogs? The newcomers might be unaware that dogs and bears do not mix, so a friendly tip might be called for.

The sun is beginning to set. Chris stops, unfolds from the driver's seat, and approaches the camper. Neither her vehicle nor her clothes suggest who she is or why she stopped.

"Hi guys." A friendly smile to head the dialogue in the right direction. A few steps towards the back of the vehicle confronts her with two middle-aged men. Clean cut, well groomed, dressed for camping and hiking in the proverbial hiker's uniform – a checkered red and black shirt, brown corduroy pants, and solid brown leather hiking boots. They are both kneeling behind the RV among a pile of tools, camping equipment, and food yet to be stowed. Neither gets up.

4

"Just got here?" she asks.

"About half an hour ago," she learns.

Not everybody enjoys a lecture about the local idiosyncrasies while setting up camp, so she puts her thumbs through the belt loop in the universal all-is-cool gesture and smiles. And she offers, "FYI: There are lots of bears around here. Waking up hungry from the recent end of their hibernation, sometimes in a nasty mood, so please don't leave the dog food or any other food outside when you retire, will ya?"

The shorter of the campers says, "Good advice. So, how big do they get?"

Good question. "Big enough to best not piss them off. And when they have cubs, the females are highly protective and ideally not trifled with."

The taller of the two says, "Do you work here?"

Interesting question, Chris thinks. "Just attended a meeting. Not my turf, actually. I am checking something on my way home." After a moment of silence, she wishes the two goodbye and climbs back into the car.

A languid cruise over the remaining road inside the campground gives Chris the time to ponder what she just came across. Other than one certifiably crazy guy on a bike who's sleeping in a really tiny tent, the RV'ers she just encountered are the only camp occupants. Late spring makes for nasty cold nights in the Jemez. Who the hell goes camping in May in the Jemez? The trip back from the rear of the grounds will lead past the RV on the way out, offering an opportunity to take a second look. Was or is there something worth a second look? Somethings out of place?

As soon as she is out of earshot, the first words out of the shorter guys mouth are, "Shit…. who the fuck was

5

that? Eager-beaver-know-it-all? Cop? Park Ranger? What do we do?" The taller one takes no more than a few seconds to offer, "We do nothing. She'll go away." The body language of both suggests a degree of alertness and unease that does not match these benign words.

Chris is coming around the loop, having found the grill and picnic table area she came to inspect for suitability for the rally. The place is a great choice, featuring abundant off-road parking, a few standard rusty, black steel Park Service charcoal grills, and enough picnic tables for a group of twenty. The only downside is the distance to the water faucet. She hangs a sign on the table closest to the road with a notice that reserves this particular picnic area for Saturday Next, nine to three, for the Rio Grande North Rally Club. Permission to occupy applied for and granted as of half an hour ago, the stamp on the sign states.

Now she can turn her attention to the trip back. Her thoughts are refocused on the RV and the two guys with the most exquisite dog food in the area. And no dog. That's what did not fit: the camper's door had been open, the steps were out, and the dog remained invisible and inaudible! Any self-respecting athletic, adult, large breed dog will show up to inspect a newcomer.

Time to run a plate check, Chris concludes. Ample reason to ask for the registration, license, and insurance. She lowers the speed a bit more, giving her more time to think and make less noise, at the same time giving the campers less time to prepare for her return visit. As she comes around the last curve, the trees and the brush between the road and the pullout with the RV lightens, and now the front of the vehicle comes into view. And low and behold, the vehicle has no front license plate. Missouri requires two plates. Chris stops to ponder the next steps. Now the time to ask for "Ze Papers Pliss" has come. Two anomalies, the dog and the missing plate, are a touch too much to simply dismiss the situation as usual. On the back of her belt, covered by her shirt, dangle a pair of handcuffs

6

old enough for the patina to have worn off. Her Smith and Wesson 357 magnum, short-barreled with no protruding hammer to catch on clothing, was in the glove box until a few seconds ago and now is in her right pants pocket. The leather document holder with the paperwork that proves that she is within her jurisdiction and for all intents and purposes a cop, is in her other pocket.

As she coasts forward, the camper now between her and the two men shields her approach and provides for a stealthy arrival. The two guys are utterly surprised when they discover Chris standing right next to them. She pulls out her identification and holds it up in the dim light.

"I'm Officer Salazar from the Santa Fe County Sheriff's Department, and I would like to see the registration, driver's license, and the insurance certificate for both vehicles." Shorty gets up without a word and walks past Chris and disappears in the camper, ostensibly to retrieve the papers, while the tall guy climbs halfway through the towed vehicle in search of the other set of documents.

Chris immediately realizes that she created a less than desirable situation, putting herself halfway between the two. Too late now. Working burglary for all her career did not instill in her the intuitive reflexes of a traffic or a vice cop. The tall guy mumbles something inaudible with his face buried inside the towed vehicle, facing away from her. As she turns and steps towards the car, he climbs back out, waves some papers at her, and says, "Here we go." Chris takes the paperwork just as he inquires, "We've been here for less than an hour. We didn't drive, spit, smoke, or drink. So, what's up?"

She is about to point out that she asks the questions here but decides to keep the conversation non-confrontational.

She never hears the short one emerge from the RV before the arrow from his crossbow pierces her from behind. A perfect, noiseless shot. Easy from three feet away. Lots of energy still in the arrow after such a short flight. She is out cold before she hits the ground. Two minutes later, she expires after her body shuts down from blood loss.

Defending the Gate

The first signs that something nefarious was underway became evident pretty much by accident. It all started on this pleasant, bright May morning.

Jason Sedillo works for Centerra, a large private security company. Jason is, such is the curse of many security personnel, a bit overweight from sitting in patrol vehicles for hours on end. Far from the ponderous personalities often seen in his business, he is reasonably sharp and observant, not wearied into dullness by an uneventful existence, personality traits highly desirable for this job.

As Jason walks through the Los Alamos Laboratory's Security Operations Center approaching the shift supervisor's office, he first comes upon a haggard-looking female assistant. She is on the phone, yet immediately recognizes Jason and signals with a thumbs-up gesture that Albert McGuigan, the supervisor on duty, should be able to see him right now.

Al's door is closed, but he waves Jason through the glass door to come in. Al had been a career officer in the U.S. Army, retiring as a Major, before signing on at Centerra as one of the seventeen shift supervisors taking turns in the SOC. The seemingly high seniority of Al and his colleagues is justified by the risks a security breach might represent, rather than the number of employees that need to be managed. Since the office is occupied around the clock by senior staff on a rotation schedule, that office is orderly, impersonal, neat, clean, and efficiently furnished.

Jason comes to a stop, standing erect three feet from the desk with his hands at his side; it's a posture that should comply with Al's expectations. And it does. It takes maybe fifteen seconds till Al looks up from whatever endless form he has been filling in on his keyboard, just long enough for Jason to signal his impatience by whipping up and down on his toes.

"What's up?" Al inquires.

The guard staff reporting to the SOC supervisor do not often come to this office, therefore the expectation is that something out of the ordinary has come up. And the ordinary on an average day is routine to the point of being boring. The largest United States Nuclear Research Facility is under constant watch, with dozens of vehicles and hundreds of officers patrolling the perimeter fence. In many ways, the patrols represent a public show of force and are intended as a deterrent. At the same time, the perimeter is actually secured by an amazing array of electronic monitoring equipment. Anybody driving the perimeter road is seen, heard, and otherwise detected and monitored for conduct unbecoming a casual visitor.

Los Alamos Laboratory is located about a forty-five-minute drive from Santa Fe, New Mexico. It is huge. Thirty-five square miles, situated in the Jemez mountains on the eastern slope of the mountain. While the Lab employs a workforce of about eleven thousand, a significant fraction of the workforce is dedicated to Lab security. The number is classified. Jason is one of that group. The manpower assigned to the United States Nuclear Weapons Program is subject to yet a tighter classification. The rest, the majority of the remainder, work on dozens of projects like Artificial Intelligence, robotics, nanotechnology, and all sorts of science and engineering projects that don't go bang.

Jason looks at the guest's chair. "This is going to take a minute or two." A finger points to the chair, and Jason sits down.

Jason, on his way here has spent a few minutes organizing his thoughts, recognizing that unstructured babble would bring an instant frown on Al's forehead rather than the attention he seeks. Jason is eager to make a mark. Promotions are infrequent. Turnover here is slow. Any break in the routine may contain an opportunity for career advancement. Time to stay sharp.

"I found a game camera attached to a tree, right opposite the gate at T.A. fifty-five. Right across the street. It is pointing at the gate." Tech Area fifty-five is part of the Lab where plutonium pits are being manufactured in a multi-billion-dollar effort to modernize the U.S. nuclear weapons inventory. T.A. fifty-five has but one gate. LANL does not refurbish the weapon itself. Refurbishment of a deployable weapon is a substantial project involving a lot of tasks beyond the work on the Pit. That additional work is being shared between Sandia Labs down in Albuquerque and Pantex in Amarillo.

A Pit is the actual fuel assembly that is consumed by nuclear fission in a horrendous fireball. But only when everything is done just right. And doing it right is tricky.

"What's a game camera?" Al is clearly not a hunter.

"As far as I could gather, there are many makes and models available; they are pretty much all the same. They consist of an infrared motion sensor that triggers a digital camera, all packaged in a waterproof, camouflaged housing."

"Who put it there and why?" Excellent question, boss, Jason thinks.

"Hunters use them throughout the year to so they know where to show up when the hunting season starts."

Jason jumps at the chance to show off his deductive capabilities.

"Neither I nor any of the others have ever seen any game at this location, nor have there been fecal droppings – at least not recently. While the road itself is very quiet, the presence of guards both inside and outside the fence would keep game from venturing to that spot. Small game, like a rabbit or small coyote won't trigger the camera. Logic dictates that this is suspicious. Until proven otherwise."

Al listened intently. "When does your shift end?"

Jason takes a look at his watch. "It ended about an hour ago. I used the computer in the standby room to Google the camera's user manual. I copied down the make, model, and serial number while trying to stay out of the lens's reach."

Al is now wide awake. He reaches for the phone and calls what Jason assumes is his boss; however, Al's side of the conversation reveals that he is talking to the assistant outside the office.

"In 45 minutes, say twelve-thirty, I will need a secure meeting room for about an hour, and get the following people: the guy from the FBI down the hall, as well as the most senior guard currently at the gate at TA-55. Have him assign a replacement from the standby room. Also, I want one of the techies with a Q security clearance – make sure it's not the guy with the red ponytail, since he doesn't know shit. And Jason as well." Just before putting the phone down he realizes that she hung up already. He yells loudly through the closed door, "And tell them to come themselves, not send some underling."

"Good work Jason. Find out what room she is getting us and be there on time."

A Faint Scent of Trouble

Everybody is on time. The seating arrangement reflects the informal seniority status, with Jason coming in on the bottom of the pyramid.

Before their arrival, Al had a chance to come up with a plan for the meeting. "Afternoon. This is important. We might have an attempt at a security breach at TA-55." All motion, fidgeting, paper shuffling, and coughing stops cold.

"Jason, why don't you walk us through what you stumbled on?" Jason gets up but is immediately signaled to sit down again since the group is only five men. Jason repeats, essentially verbatim, what he told Al before the meeting. Al offers that there might be an innocent explanation, but for the time being, this should be treated as a threat.

"Ok guys: this is need-to-know only. It could be an inside job. Let us come up with the next few steps. Until I say different, all interactions outside of this group will be done through me. I will leave a briefing note for the late afternoon shift supervisor. Now let's have some ideas."

The appearance of the five is a dead giveaway as to their role. The FBI is dressed as expected; he did, however, leave his jacket in his office and arrived in a crisp white long-sleeved shirt. The FBI is permanently conducting interviews for security clearance applicants, and he acts and dresses the part. The techie is in beige slacks, Birkenstocks and a golf shirt. Both Jason and the guy from the Gate are in uniform, with the usual flashlight, a Taser, and a .45 hanging off their belt. Al looks more like an engineer than a retired army major and is in a short-sleeved tan shirt.

The FBI agent speaks first. "Could obviously be a hunter. It could be spooks. It could be press. It could be one of the crazies that hate nukes. It doesn't make a bean's worth of difference. We have to determine who and why. In such a way that the source of the device is not privy to the fact that we are on to him."

We are with you. Brilliant deductive capability demonstrated in the most obvious manner, Al concludes.

Al wants to know how long the batteries are supposed to last. Not without pride, Jason offers that the manual claims battery life to be between three and four months.

Al frowns. "So, periodically, but probably not less often than every second month, someone shows up, changes out the batteries and the chip with the pictures. How the hell is this done without the guards noticing? How come we spend tens of millions on security, and we find this by stumbling over it? How long has the damn thing been there?"

It's the FBI's turn again.

"Let's order the same camera with a bunch of spare chips and batteries. Let us become familiar with the functionality and the limitations." It turns out that the FBI guy's name is Matt Murphy. He takes a deep breath; he is used to listening, not talking much.

Techie has no comment for the time being. Perhaps because he is busy locating the second Birkenstock that slipped from his foot.

Jason suggests that approaching the tree-mounted camera from behind should make it possible to cover the lens and then remove, copy, and reinstall the chip. Al immediately sees the flaw in this plan and proposes to temporarily replace the hostile camera with the to-be-purchased unit so that the Lab can dust for prints and collect DNA, if the owners were stupid enough to leave any behind. Right afterward, the original camera will go back to where it was found. He adds, "Have the Lab check for prints on the batteries – wiping the batteries clean of prints is often missed."

Al is way ahead of the others. It's clear that this is either what he hopes for, namely nothing – or this is pretty scary. It might potentially be scary because of the implications of someone watching when, who, how, and what is coming out of that gate.

Al offers his spontaneous thoughts. "If the camera has been there for a while, multiple visits have gone undetected. This implies that the individual that installed the device may have come up from the ravine. Let's make sure that we do not change our routine nor our procedures."

Now, finally, FBI is eager to contribute.

"Experience shows that it's tricky to discover a watcher and set up surveillance without it being noticed. While one is still in the dark as to who is observing whom and for what reason, it's best to change as little as possible and keep the circle of those in the know as small as possible."

Al seems eager to wrap up the meeting and he shuts down FBI with a curt "Let's get cracking. As discussed."

Is the Arrow Broken?

Al is in a quandary. He alone, among this meetings attendees is familiar with the ready-made plans in case of a security breach. So, how much do I disclose, he wonders?

The loss or the theft of any nuclear weapon or any components thereof triggers a response that is as much driven by paranoia about an actual risk of an explosion as it is about an impending public relations disaster. The condition when nukes are compromised is referred to as Broken Arrow. Very symbolic, easy to remember, and scary as hell. As one would expect, this condition initiates a series of activities taken by very senior military personnel and top-level scientists, using the prepared playbook.

Not long after the alarm bells are silenced, the planners and scientists are rushed to a previously determined assembly point, while equipment and personnel, vehicles, and aircraft of all sorts and sizes follow right behind. The ARG (Broken Arrow) Accident Response Group, unfortunately, has had past opportunities to practice a few real emergencies and a series of endless drills. Much of the equipment they carry is unique to their operational assignment, items ranging from airtight suits that remind one of the moon landings, down to brooms and buckets for the decontamination of spills involving radioactive isotopes.

Full deployment of the ARG is what Al had solicited. Premature and overkill, he was told by those who must grant permission. "All you have, so far, is an unexplained game camera. Bring us proof of an impending attempt of an attack, and you can have the Army, the Navy, and the Air Force. Right now, all you get is a small, justifiable sized, team."

In this instance, the place chosen as the assembly point for the few military personnel, the scientists, and the ground vehicles is the National Guard Armory in Santa Fe, a good 45-minute drive away from the Lab. The aircraft, a fixed-wing Citation, and a Blackhawk helicopter flew to the National Guard Hangars at the Santa Fe airport. For a good reason: every attempt is made to keep the public in the dark that something is afoot.

The discovery of the game camera near the gate at the Lab's perimeter leads to a seemingly endless discussion about who is trying to do what to whom. The conclusion that vehicles transporting nuclear components might be the most probable target is finally settled on.

A constant need for moving weapons and weapon parts has led to the creation of an organization specializing for just that one job. The Office of Secure Transportation, called OST, currently part of the Department of Energy, has its transportation control center, TEC, at Kirtland AFB in Albuquerque. Much of the movement of OST's trips are between Labs, secure storage, and workshops, such as

LANL in Los Alamos, Sandia in Albuquerque, and Pantex in Amarillo. Non-descript, unmarked tractor-trailers called "Safeguard Transporters," lead and followed discreetly by unmarked, ever-changing civilian trucks and cars, move their deadly cargo, just about always without incident.

When Pits need to be moved between the various locations involved in the refurbishment efforts, the extent of the security effort involved largely depends on the number of Pits moved. Moving multiple units involves the full OST protocol; when the move is restricted to one or two units, a non-descript minivan with no armed escort is the preferred method. In these cases, they occur infrequently, discretion is thought to be more effective than a weapons transfer with highly visible security.

Harry and His Airport

It's early in the morning. The air is still brisk and does not yet give a hint of the heat that I will face around noontime.

My dog is fed, I enjoyed a healthy breakfast and I am looking forward to today's flight. The time has come to go to work, assuming that flying for a living can be considered work.

Santa Fe airport doesn't really wake up till about seven in the morning, and it's just about six now. I have the place mostly to myself.

I left my helicopter out on the ramp last night since I landed way too late to work on it in the dimly lit hangar. Now I need to clean the dead bugs off the huge bubble, calculate how much fuel I'll need, have her fueled, do a pre-flight inspection, and complete yesterday's paperwork. And I will prepare today's pre-flight documents and stuff an envelope sealed with today's flight plan that I will mail to myself as proof that I did everything I am supposed to do before defying gravity. Just in case something goes wrong and the FAA comes breathing down my neck, under the predictable assumption that I did not dot the i's or cross the t's.

But the bugs come first since they will be a bitch to remove once the sun starts heating the bubble.

Jack drives the fuel truck up and wanders off to get the generator since he knows that I have an aging battery that will need an external powered start. The aging onboard battery requires at least twenty minutes of charging after takeoff, and I will be on the way to my destination for just about fifteen minutes. A new battery can provide three starts, best case. And the new battery has been back-ordered for three weeks now. From where I am heading, I can't walk back to the airport or I wouldn't be flying there in the first place; thus, I need to leave here fully charged. The life of an aviator can be challenging.

Today's flight involves a few trips back and forth between the airport and small sandy islands in the middle of the Rio Grande on a stretch of the river with no access other than by helicopter or by donkey.

When I got the call requesting a quote, I was told that a photo crew and four or five models will show up at eight in the morning for a fashion shoot. Back on Tuesday, when the call came in, I instantly and joyfully visualized the arrival of a few Tens and one or maximum two Nines, as well as the photo crew's assorted unshaven males with ponytails.

I like predictable customers. No such luck this time, as I am about to find out.

It's seven-thirty. The photo crew pulls up in a Ryder's rental. Three clean-shaven mid-thirties guys get out. Two disappear behind the truck, and I hear the banging noises that I assume are associated with hauling Pelican cases with the camera gear out of the back.

The driver walks over.

As he gets closer, I say, "Doctor Livingstone, I presume?" No discernable response. Obviously not a history buff. I try a less sophisticated approach.

He has a mid-Atlantic accent. "Morning. I hope you don't mind us being a bit early. The girls will arrive in about forty-five minutes. Separate van. Figured you might want to run us and the gear up to the shot location and then come back for the models."

I offer what I hope is a winning smile. He doesn't wait, and an outstretched hand holds an envelope that I sincerely hope is for the check I was promised. It goes into my back pocket.

"Harry," I say as I shake his hand. Sturdy grip, tanned arms. He's taller than me by about two inches.

"John. Peter and Mike are unloading."

"Mighty thoughtful of you. Meaning the check and being early. Let's chat for a minute about today."

He glances at the helicopter.

"Long Ranger? Seven seats?"

"Yep. Tell me, how much does your gear weigh? Your production assistant told me your cargo will be 190 pounds in four boxes. That sound about right?"

"Dead on. Nine-hundred- and fifty-pounds total."

I am satisfied. He's done this before. I figure the girls will weigh six hundred and fifty for all five and less than one hundred pounds for the garments.

Flight time one way is fifteen minutes plus another twenty for finding the perfect spot for the camera and another island for the models. The camera operator will tell me when we get there how far the lens and the models have to be distanced.

Burning the first hour giving a ride to the crew and the gear will leave me with an hour and a half, plenty for ferrying the girls up and back with ample reserve once the shot is done, giving the crew time to pack up for their return. Done by sunset. Cool.

I work off my mental checklist for a movie or a photoshoot. "You got water? Food? Chemical potty? A tent for the girls to change in?" He nods: water and food. "We are good." No tent. So, they will change clothes in the open? Wonderful. The day is getting better by the minute.

We Meet Mike and John

The camera gear has been stowed, and they're all strapped in. John sits in the co-pilot seat. It's just before eight. The doors are closed.

I see Jack walking up to the generator. Reputation has it that he does have eyes in the back of his head, and the fact that he noticed me getting ready is ample proof of that. My thumb goes up, and I can see the generator starting to belch black smoke and then settle down to a steady hum. He glances at me, and my index finger replaces the thumb as I make a circular motion. Let her rip. Jack flips the switch on the side of the generator, and the cockpit comes alive. The master warning buzzes; there is nothing wrong – the buzzer merely is delivering proof that it works. I silence it.

Time to start with the checklist. I mumble to myself as I work my way down the list.

*Rotor untied, flight controls free and correct and posi-
tioned for start, friction lock set. Throttle closed. Engine anti-ice
Off. Hydraulics boost On. Particle separator Off.*

I ensure that all instruments show static at zero.
Someone in the back is fidgeting around and we rock gently on the skids. John stares straight ahead watching a
Cessna Citation Jet arrive with the nose in the flare a bit
too high off the ground. Is John a pilot? Is that why he noticed?

*Strobe lights on, circuit breakers on. Six of the caution
lights are lit. Turbine outlet temperature light press to test. Caution lights press to test, and all come on. Fuel quantity check.*

We are getting there. My left hand checks that the
collective is all the way down.

*The rotor is clear. Fuel boost goes On, and caution lights
go out, fuel pressure comes up.*

Let's fire up the engine.

I start the timer. I engage the starter, and I have less
than forty seconds for a start, or I will fry the starter. Those
boys cost as much as a small car. As I hit the starter, I can
hear the ignition click away. I hear the generator lose
speed under load and quickly recover.

Once the turbine is spinning at twelve percent, I introduce fuel, and I am immediately rewarded with a *pouf*
as the fuel catches fire. I modulate the throttle in the yellow arc. The main rotor starts turning. I see the oil pressure
increasing. I release the starter at fifty-eight percent turbine rpm. Time to give the starter-generator a minute to
cool down. The onboard generator comes online. A hand
signal to Jack shuts down the external generator. I switch
the Radio Master On.

The headset squeals, and I inquire, "Are you guys ready?" and I get three prompt and affirmative responses.

I tune the radio to the information frequency.

".... automated weather observation 1-2-1-5 ZULU. Wind 220 at 18. Visibility 10. Sky condition clear. Temperature is 22. Dewpoint is minus 5. Altimeter 3-0-01. Remarks: Density altitude 8200. Runaway in use is two zero. Contact ground on 121.7 with information Bravo."

A glance at the instruments shows everything in the green. I set the altimeter to the field setting. Time to go to work. The throttle goes to full. I raise the collective until I can feel that she is getting light on the skids, followed by lifting the helicopter into a low hover.

The miracle of heavier-than-air flight never gets old.

I squeeze the transmit button. "Santa Fe Tower, good morning, November 19 Echo Alpha with Bravo ready for a westbound departure."

Bob comes right back with "19 Echo Alpha you are cleared takeoff from present position; stay below seven thousand until three miles west for traffic now joining downwind."

I stare out of the bubble but can't find it yet. I acknowledge, "Echo Alpha is cleared to depart westbound below seven requesting a call once we are past the traffic."

A helicopter transitioning from a hover to a cruise-climb is a thing of beauty, smooth and elegant, and I need yet again remind myself that getting paid for this is the cherry on the cake. As everybody who tried it did discover that helicopter flying is more an art than a science. It's terrifying when you are a green student, it's rewarding once you get good at it. Learning to hover is what cleanses the gene pool. That is incorrect: it is hitting wires that is even more problematic.

New Mexico gets rural in one hell of a hurry. Three minutes after takeoff, we are out there among the Chamisas, the rocks, the cactus, and the rattlesnakes. The only vegetation that reliably survives out here – other than the rocks and the cactus - is pinon and a low shrubby juniper. The ground is covered with coarse sand since very little organic material ever deteriorates into what is elsewhere considered soil. No water, no nutrients: hence sparse vegetation – hence no soil.

The terrain climbs for a bit, and then the flight descends towards Lake Cochiti. This artificial lake acts as a buffer and a reservoir for the agricultural use of Rio Grande water from here on south to Albuquerque.

Most of the year, the Rio Grande is not that grand at all. It's a narrow, shallow, muddy river that will start to earn its grandiose name much further down south as it winds itself through Texas and Mexico into the Gulf of Mexico. Way up here it is, other than wells, the only source of water. Period. An oversimplified reality states that in New Mexico you don't buy land, you buy water rights – ownership of the land is a fringe benefit.

Lake Cochiti is at a low water level, as usual. The moment you turn right up the mouth of the river, all access other than by boat or by air will cease to exist. The river winds itself between sheer walls of rock north for a few miles.

About halfway between Cochiti and the nearest bridge across the Rio Grande near the next native American pueblo, the Bandelier National Monument boundary ends in the middle of the river at just about the spot where the Los Alamos National Lab Restricted Airspace area also shares that boundary. Flying into the airspace over a

National Park is off-limits. So is flying into Restricted Airspace. Why is this relevant? Because the Parks Service employs a wide range of talent, ranging from friendly, warm, and knowledgeable to totally anal and challenging. The latter sort doesn't staff the pay booths at the park entrance – the difficult ones work an office job and many see their mission in life in harassing anyone NOT working for the federal government.

Where we are heading, all land other than the Lab's and the Park belongs to the Bureau of Land Management. The BLM subscribes to a similar work ethic as the Park Service. I was shocked to hear that the BLM has its own armed police force. The theft of public lands must be a considerable problem, though I have yet to hear of a single case.

Once the jurisdiction changes to the Lab, the situation changes dramatically.

The Lab was built in the middle of nowhere back during the Manhattan Project, back when the first Nuclear Weapon was developed. Its landmass is enormous. The boundaries of the Lab itself are well protected, since a significant fraction of the Lab's workforce is dedicated to securing all access points. Innocuous looking white SUVs can be seen on all the perimeter roads. The place on the river I am aiming for is just outside the borders of both LANL's restricted airspace and the Bandelier Park.

Los Alamos is a small town with some unique features: a very high average household income (often both parents work at high-paying jobs at the Lab) and many of their children are inevitably overachievers and they get to walk into any Ivy League university they desire. Los Alamos draws from one exceptional gene pool.

We are slowly creeping up the river, a few feet above the water right in the center between the two shallow river banks. Every few hundred feet, there are sandy islands that stick out of the water by mere inches, and these islands are always moving as the river brings new sand and gravel and relocates existing islands downstream a few feet at a time.

I know this river well. I am pretty sure that the spot I am heading for is still there, mostly unchanged and just what is needed for today's shot. And what I need are two islands, a few hundred feet apart, sunlit till about three o'clock, with the northmost island having a tree lying across the sand, suitable for hiding the garments that will continuously be exchanged and protected from the camera's view as the shoot progresses.

I slow down as we turn the last bend in the river. Back when I submitted my offer for this charter I had pointed out exactly where I was going to take the client, as documented by an attached satellite image.

"John: you like the island right before us for the cameras? And the island just beyond that for the models?" John is visualizing the next few hours, the sunlight, the shadows, the protection from airliner contrails offered by the high walls, and he concedes that this will work. I float a few feet off the water and come to a low hover.

I stop my descent a few inches off the sand, right at the closer end of the island with the helicopters tail sticking out over the river, so as to leave a lot of space for the equipment and the crew.

I look at John, and he nods. I let the skids settle on the wet sand. I have found the camera crew a home for the next few hours. The throttle is closing, the rotor blades slow down, and I let the timer run for two minutes as the engine cools down, and then I shut the engine down so they can unload.

Girls, Girls, Girls

I am almost back at the airport. It's now past eight, and the camera crew and the gear has been left behind on the island.

Bob, the controller, welcomes me back, and I land right next to a sizeable black minivan on the ramp. I see four casually dressed females watching me land. The fifth is just emerging from the general aviation terminal, walking towards me and tucking her shirt into a pair of delightfully tight shorts.

During the cool down, I have ample time to check out the models. No Nines and no Tens. Sixes and maybe a Seven. Doing a photoshoot in such a problematic shot location for what I was told is a fashion catalog for the fall and winter season using such average looking models seems like overkill – but then it ain't my dough.

A male climbs out of the driver seat of the van. I recognize him, but do not remember his name. He's pulling a few bags that look like Navy sea sacks out of the cargo space in the rear of the van. These bags with the garments will just barely fit into the cargo hold of the helicopter.

Not knowing the passengers, and their propensity to walk into a spinning tail rotor, I shut down the engine, and once the main rotor blades stop turning, I swing my legs out and lower myself to the ground.

Since it will get hot just a few hours from now, I remove the front doors of the aircraft and load them onto the back of the fuel truck that's just now arriving for an unsolicited top-off. I wave him away since I am weary of dragging around lots of extra fuel, despite the old adage that the only time one has too much fuel is when the aircraft is on fire.

"Good morning." The response is timid. A smile here, a smile there. Downcast eyes. They saunter over and peek inside. Five seats are in the rear cabin, and one is next to me where John sat a few minutes ago. I am eager to find out who feels drawn toward the seat in the front next to the open door. Will it be the most assertive girl, the one that wants the view, or will it be the one that hesitated longest and is now stuck with having to sit half-way outside in the airflow? I am loading the bags into the cargo bay in the back, while the seating arrangements are negotiated without much dialogue. I am blessed with Hotpants climbing into the left front seat.

In the back, I hear four seat belts click closed, and the headsets are being donned with no visible worries about damage to the carefully arranged hairdo. This is no feature movie we will be shooting, there will be no close-up shots, and therefore the usual hair, wardrobe, and makeup staff are not present. The girls will be on their own, getting instructions via a two-way radio. I assume that will be John's responsibility.

As we leave, I explain where we are going and some of the logistics relating to drop-off. I never fail to warn about the perils of walking into a spinning tail-rotor. I explain that after they are on the second island and once the bags are off, that I will move the helicopter back to the island with the camera crew and shut down. I plan to become a casual yet interested observer. After all: they have no tent to change in.

As we approach the island I have set aside for the models, I see that the camera crew has successfully set up their gear and are ready to start taking pictures just as soon as the girls are in place. The last hundred feet of the flight takes us out over the river and avoids the first island so as to ensure that the camera gear, now set up on tripods, will not get caught in the rotor downdraft and disappear into the shallow water.

The distance between the two islands is probably two hundred feet. On the island where the models are setting up, there is no artificial lighting, so we have to live with what sunlight is available until the shot is done. For that reason alone, I am in a bit of a hurry to get the helicopter, after unloading the passengers and the garment bag, as efficiently as possible out of the shot by repositioning the aircraft back behind the camera crew.

Now I can relax and watch the events unfold.

John has lent a two-way radio to the models, who are too far away to shout over the sound of the river water flowing by. I can't hear the voices without a radio, yet I find it easy to piece together what is going on and give meaning to the mimed performance.

What I observe is a repetitive cycle that starts with radio traffic, followed by the models changing into the next to be photographed outfit. The moments where the girls change is not as rewarding as I anticipated, due to the distance between my position behind the camera team and the girls on their island. The models are ordered around to catch the right light and to compose what is supposed to be an artistically pleasing arrangement. It all seems a bit amateurish. The cameraman seems to know what he is doing. The models, however, must have gotten hired straight from their evening jobs as cocktail waitresses. John is attentive to the job, so is the cameraman, but the other guy seems more interested in studying the beautiful scenery. He keeps looking up at the sheer cliffs that seem to descend straight into the edge of the river. Just about where this is all taking place, a ravine, overgrown with brush, ascends steeply in the general direction of the plateau above. It ends up on the plateau near the Bandelier entrance, close to the Los Alamos Lab. I know this part of the area like the back of my hand.

At some point, as the sun starts to creep behind the edge of the tall cliffs above, the shoot is declared a success. I wake up from a brief nap that I took, sitting in the more comfortable seats in the back of the helicopter.

The morning's flight sequence is reversed; first, the models get delivered back to the airport, and then the camera team gets picked up and flown to the same destination.

By seven, I on my way back to take a shower and change. Time to take a friend to dinner.

The Sheriff is Missing a Deputy

The phone rings three times before it is yanked from the cradle. The young lady whose job it is to interact with the law enforcement community at the Lab has a habit of taking her own sweet time to say something – anything – while she is hunting for a pen, and then she belts out "This Is Marcy at Law Enforcement Support how can I help you" in one continuous breathless announcement.

"Hi. This is Sergeant Edwards from the Santa Fe County Sheriff's Office. Glad to hear that this was the right number. But I have no idea who to talk to, and perhaps you can get me to the right individual."

Pause. He continues.

"We have a missing person situation. This time it's one of our own that has gone missing. The reason I'm calling you is the now established fact that the last time she was seen was at the headquarters of Bandelier National Monument, right in your backyard."

Marcy says, "… I am new here, don't know the protocol yet, but I can get a message into the system. Who's missing?"

"Ok. Here's what we know: about a week ago, Christine Salazar was last seen leaving the headquarters of Bandelier after a staff meeting. Two days later, she did not show up for work – no reason was given. Friday a week ago, Chris, who had been tasked with organizing a car rally for the staff, was supposed to hang a reservation sign, and she did. In the end, she didn't show up at that rally, however. She's a volunteer deputy with this office. Hasn't been home since. Her cat was really thirsty once we checked up on her. We listened to her voice mail, and the oldest message was from the day after she was at that staff meeting. She's thirty-nine years old, five-five, about 135 pounds, short brown hair, drives a dark blue civilian Honda Camry, license plate . . . ohhhh crap I'll call you back with that . . . and she lives in Nambe. Are we good so far?"

"Sure. But slow down a bit. I am typing an email as you speak."

"Sure. Sorry. Now, we're aware that you have extensive camera surveillance at the perimeter road and we're hoping that you might be able to help establish when and how Chris proceeded home; going home was what she told the others she was doing when she left. The current assumption being that she might never have gotten there. The case is being investigated by Detective Martinez, who is out right now and told me to ask for your help."

"Anything else?"

"Whoever is going to look into this can reach me at extension 1201 or Martinez on his cell – his number will follow in an email, together with her license plate. I'll also send over the only picture we have from her badge, not very flattering, but possibly helpful nevertheless. Give me an email address."

"I'll call you back with that, once we know who will deal with this."

"One more thing: her cell last pinged close to where she parked her car during the meeting at Bandelier. Her battery might have run out. Or she might have lost it close to there. T-Mobile tells us cell reception along that back road is intermittent."

Marcy promises to find the right individual and either have that person call back with the contact info or call back herself.

Mister Smith Meets Senior Gonzales

Mexicans generally are very friendly and accommodating people. Those who have been treated with either indifference or hostility by gringo tourists have been known to hold a grudge and might be inclined to follow their lower instincts. Give them credit: taking a walk at night in a dark alley of a rural Mexican town by a tourist shows a lack of judgment justifiably punishable by a mugging. Dark alleys in Mexico are a touch safer than the back streets of Manhattan – but still!

The visitor from Santa Fe had arrived by train, the famous El Chepe, originating out of Chihuahua, starving and thirsty. The train was cheaper and slower than a flight, and it had the added advantage of getting him to Los Mochis without leaving a paper trail. After checking in at the hotel and dropping his bag, he ventured out, and following the receptionist's suggestion, he turned right toward the bright lights in search of nourishment.

He looks up at the intersection where he is informed that the hotel is on Hidalgo, intersected by Juarez street. Immediately the old joke about the gringo with zero command of Spanish who tells the cab driver that he wants to go back to Hidalgo and Una Via – one-way street – comes to mind.

The cuisine south of the border is vastly different region by region. On the Pacific coast, the sensible thing to do is to go for seafood. Beef in Mexico, he knows, both from experience and by reputation, compares poorly with Prime Beef from north of the border. What a Mexican would call a steak, cut about a quarter-inch thick, would be listed under appetizers as capriccio in Texas. The second cantina he encounters has their menu hanging in the entrance. They specialize in what comes from the sea.

He seeks a table facing the entrance door, next to a table with three Americans. The substantial number of empty beer bottles is a good indication that they have not come off the same train as himself; there simply was not enough time for each to drink three bottles of Pacifico. Maybe.

Howdy's are exchanged, and as both tables start to interpret the menu, a joint effort to narrow down the options develops quickly.

"*Pescado* is Spanish for fish, correct?"

"That covers a fair range doesn't it? Ranges from a minnow to Moby Dick, so we better ask." No one points out that Moby Dick is a mammal.

The three men must have very divergent backgrounds; the know-it-all among the group wearing a birder's hat, discovered *pulpo* and spontaneously burst into a lecture revealing the length and width of his wisdom.

"I've always been intrigued by the conflict among scholars about the plural of Octopus. The standard English plural of Octopus is Octopuses. However, the word octopus comes from Greek, and the Greek plural form is Octopodes. The modern usage of Octopodes is so infrequent that many people mistakenly create the erroneous plural form Octopi, formed according to rules for Latin plurals."

Eyes are being discreetly raised to heaven as the show-off is allowed to briefly dwell on his wisdom.

The engineer among the group, the guy with the plastic pocket protector on his shirt, shall not be outdone and offers, "So, two Octopuses are one hexapus?" His wit is rewarded with a grin from those within English language earshot. At least all of those that had pursued higher education with either a Greek or an Information Technology major.

A filet of *mero*, or grouper in English, rice, black beans, and roasted plantains paired with a cup of garlic butter shows up pretty quickly. A Pacifico washes it down.

He takes great pains to keep the unavoidable conversation steered towards food, away from "where are you from," "what brings you here," and "how long do you stay in Los Mochis?" In response to the first such question, he shovels a big heap of beans into his mouth; this blocks his ability to answer and inhibits further conversation for a while.

Any self-respecting document or comment about Los Mochis on the Pacific coast of Mexico will point out that the copper cannon railroad begins or ends here in this not terribly attractive town that is the center of illegal drug distribution for the West Coast of the USA. Mister Smith – let's call him that for the moment – knows that. Homework. El Chapo, probably the most recognizable drug lord ever, is from here. Tourists may come and go, and few stay longer than necessary. Those that linger may take a day's side trip to Alamos, two hours away, in the hills before the terrain takes a steep climb up the central highlands. Alamos is every bit the sweet Mexican town, sleepy, full of narrow street with cobblestones, not discovered by fat cat gringos till about a decade ago. By now, the old archetypal Farmer in the white pajama and the sombrero has been replaced by the slick young real estate broker who learned the English language and his salesmanship while living, probably as an illegal, in California or Arizona. He will be praising the opportunity for the mother of all laidback lifestyles and a shot at significant economic gains by investing in a pre-construction hacienda-style condo. Even the most innocent or ignorant gringo will ultimately learn the pitfalls of giving a third-world developer upfront money to build what the funds are earmarked for. The sane method is to wait till first the builder and then the initial developer have gone insolvent and then buy from owner number three. The price will have gone up, but the risk will have gone down.

Los Mochis, on the other hand, has neither the charm nor the waterfront for anything other than container shipping, commercial fishing, and of course, the drug trade.

After a short walk back to the hotel, the visitor spends a delightful few hours recovering from the train ride.

It's just about ten in the morning when Juan Rodriguez's cellphone rings with a call from a cellphone with a 505-area code Senor Rodriguez has never been in contact with. How does he know that? He consistently enters the name of all new callers forever linking the name with the number.

In order to conceal his identity, leaving the option that a mere underling had answered the call (and thus retain deniability,) he responds with "Dig a me." Talk to me. Rude and efficient. On a cellphone, although it's a digital transmission, it is entirely possible to guess as to how far the call is coming from, based on signal delay, background noise, and other subtle indicators. The caller, the called concluded, is—little doubt here—in the general area.

Juan Rodriguez defends drug dealers, smugglers, and growers in Mexican courts. It's a lucrative business, and he represents just about always the single legal tip of a vast illegal iceberg. He gets paid offshore and is smart enough always to declare and document his income. He pays every centavo due in taxes while—legally, based on client-lawyer privilege—keeping the identity of his real client who pays his bills secret. Those that he has the privilege to represent under Mexican jurisprudence are seldom more than foot soldiers, mules, drivers, and guards. Sometimes they got caught by accident, like running a red light or parking in the direction opposing traffic, which in Mexico is a severe breach of the law since Pancho Villa's reign. At other times the defendants had been cultivated by the cartel to be fed to corrupt cops and prosecutors acting as the lions. A distraction to make the corrupt officials look good.

Notwithstanding all this camouflage, he is in the center of a complicated game. In essence, Rodriguez is keenly aware of who is up to what and with whom. The DEA is watching his office and his residence, and the residence of both his girlfriends, and they tap every one of his phones, the one's they know of. The DEA also bugged everything he touches and they put trackers in his cars. To their chagrin, they learn very little in return for all the tax dollars wasted on this operation. Over time the tricks used by the cartels to sustain such discretion have changed. Flying to some Caribbean tax haven with no bilateral extradition agreement, after nine-eleven, no longer works. By now, communications with the Chapo's of this world make use of more sophisticated and more cost-effective techniques, like encrypting text and embedding the code in the metadata of random pictures of anything or everything. Burner phones, cheap, low functionality cellphones with prepaid minutes, ready to be run over by a car, and tossed in a public garbage bin after one call are more useful than long walks on the beach, even with everyone in swim trucks with no place to hide a tracker or a bug.

Rodriguez's phone goes to speaker mode. A gringo's voice, undeniable accent, says, "Hi, my name is Peter Smith. I am calling because I understand that you represent Pablo Gonzales's business and legal interests in Mexico." No reply or response. Deniability on principal. "I am trying to find a secure way to get a message with a business proposal to Senior Gonzales."

Long pause, a polite little cough to gain time, to think.

The lawyer's near accent-free reply in English is, "Type up a teaser, no more than two hundred words and hand it to my paralegal. Her name is Patricia, last name Calderon; she is in a second-floor office at the municipal court every day till four-thirty." The call ends. Rude and efficient.

Smith is pleased. He finishes with, "My proposal will be there later this afternoon.", not realizing that the line had gone dead by now

The hotel has a business center, consisting of two old PCs and one inkjet printer. The keyboard turns out to be the usual challenge for a gringo because most keys have lost their painted letters and symbols to thousands of dirty fingertips. Keys that even at their prime are located in unexpected spots on the keyboard, prone to drive those ignorant of Hispanic keyboard layouts stir crazy. Such are the downsides of having to fit all sorts of extra characters on the same basic 103 button keyboards. Many a tourist has given up, using foul language, after futile attempts at printing boarding passes down south of the border. It takes Smith all of two hours. Now the text is ready for a silent readback.

"My name is Peter Smith. For the time being. This is a proposal for a mutually beneficial business opportunity. I represent a small group of well qualified entrepreneurs. We are aware of losses your import-export business has sustained at some northern border crossings. Press reports imply that you had invested extensively in transportation infrastructure. We furthermore understand that you lost men, equipment, export type goods, and cash to United States agencies interfering with your business interests.

We have developed a plan to recoup most or some of these losses. A relatively small cash investment is required. We are eager to present you with a draft plan of action at your earliest convenience. If this is of interest to you and your associates, please call or text my cell with instructions. Time and discretion are of the essence. Your truly P. Smith."

He leaves off the name and the cell number. Just in case the message falls into the wrong hands – for instance, a gringo who does not dress the tourism part and has a flat top crew cut, one that draws a federal paycheck. The lawyer will find the number to call on his cell. When approaching a crook with a proposition, always display robust operational security.

He finds Patricia with more ease than the courthouse. She is chubby, elderly, a bit slow, and not at all what he expected. What was expected is a tall, attractive young woman with long, tanned, slender legs. Let's assume that ol chubby here is a relative of a relative that needed a job? As Peter, name subject to change, approaches her, envelope in hand, it is evident that she has been alerted, and he was expected. She mumbles some

Spanish that he would not understand anyway, takes the envelope, turns it front and back a few times, and without another word puts it in a canvas courier pouch at her feet. The phone on the bench next to her rings, and as she answers the call and begins a rapid-fire conversation, she dismisses him with a wave of her other hand. So, we have learned that being rude is company policy. Efficiency, maybe not so much.

It's almost precisely two hours later that his phone rings. A male voice, free of any detectable accent in his English, does not wait for any opening pleasantries nor offers any says "Patricia has an envelope for you" and hangs up. Rude and efficient. Solid operational security. So far, so good. Any day, when an approach is made, with no introduction or previous contact or any displayable credentials, to a major drug lord without getting shot at, is a good day.

Peter realizes that the time left to make it to the courthouse in time is tightening up real fast and the fast walk or near run that gets him into the second-floor hall where Patricia is still sitting, leaves him panting and steaming. Anyone who spends much of one's time in the high desert with near-zero humidity, then runs around the tropics in a long sleeve shirt will tend to do that.

As Peter approaches Patricia, a hand emerges from below the desk with the same envelope, the hotel's markings clearly an indication of that. The envelope contains a different letter, brief and concise, as a first cursory glance reveals.

He reads silently.

"A black Ford Excursion will be waiting in front of your hotel tomorrow at ten. Please, no cellphones, wires, or weapons. No pens, notebooks, nothing electronic at all. Wear slacks and a white short-sleeve shirt and carry last weeks' *Time Magazine* from the hotel shop. Be on time."

So; they know where he is staying but not what he looks like. How the fuck did they figure that out in a few hours?

It's now nine-fifty in the morning. Dressed as requested, instructed is the better term, Peter reclines in the most uncomfortable chair in the lobby of the hotel, close to the train station. The airport in Los Mochis is way out of town with nothing around, no hotels, no rental car agencies. Nada. The train station was the best area in which to submerge this particular gringo in an anonymous crowd.

At five after ten, a dusty Ford with two well-dressed, but tough looking guys arrives; the driver remains at the wheel, the wingman gets out, opens the door behind the copilot seat, and silently motions the guest to hop in. Within seconds the car slides into morning traffic. No one says a word as the car heads towards the edge of town. Not more than five minutes into the drive, the vehicle stops, the guest's door is pulled open, and his presence is required outside. Despite the reluctance felt under such circumstances, he steps out. Wingman signals that raising one's arms above the head for a pat-down is now the correct thing to do. Anything you wish, senor, anything at all.

The pat-down is thorough and respectful, although there is no way to hide the kind of artillery one would want to carry for the upcoming meeting. A dark canvas bag is retrieved from the front seat and ends up over his head just as a pair of cold handcuffs snap close behind his back. Getting back into the back seat is aided by the hand on the visitor's head to keep from bumping the door sill. After the door closes, the door on the other rear seat opens, and he can feel the weight of the wingman joining them.

The whole exercise is done professionally, calmly, and in a non-threatening manner. With a blindfold on, it is impossible to determine where the car is heading. The road is smooth, and there are no topes, the nasty speed bumps the Mexicans adore so much. A few turns that feel like off- and on-ramp cloverleaves, a stop sign at an intersection that can be identified by cross-traffic that blasts past. After thirty minutes or so, a turn and they are leaving the asphalt behind, going across a cattle guard onto a dirt road, then through a gate whose hinge begs for a drop of oil.

Not one word has been exchanged. The handcuffs have started to dig into his flesh when the car comes to a halt on gravel. Once the door is open, the smell is very different from the low coast, an air cooler and drier that implies a higher elevation. His elbows are gripped firmly on either side as he is whisked up a few steps into yet a cooler place. The handcuffs come off, the hood is yanked from his head. He is barely able to determine that he is in what seems to be the entry hall into one of the hacienda-style mansions, the prolonged darkness of the trip is still blinding him as gradually his sight returns to normal. Then, as a polite gesture his vision is allowed to return to near normal, and he then takes a few steps up some stairs, where he is ushered into a large, dark, air-conditioned room.

A desk that would do well in the Oval Office is situated on the far wall of the room. A swarthy man in his forties, Armani suit, crocodile leather boots from Lucchese, no glasses, no mustache, gets up. Every effort has been made to create the appearance of a pedigree that would be the envy of the Great Gatsby. The only way to make the setting more transparent would be a brass plaque that says Drug Lord.

"Welcome. Let's sit over here," is supported by a finger pointing to a set of opposing sofas' that swallows both men up to their ear lobes. In a dark corner of the vast room is a desk, near the entrance to the room and hidden halfway behind the open by-panel door. An elderly, gray-haired man remains seated, writing on a yellow, lined legal pad. The seating arrangements have been chosen well; the host's face is difficult to see since he is backlit, facing both the visitor and the fellow in the dark corner whose assignment, one assumes, is to take notes. An inquiring look by the host must have received a positive response. The note-taker is ready.

The older fellow's haircut, way too perfect for this neighborhood, a crisp white shirt paired with a simple dark, and well-cut suit are the only remarkable observations possible in the dim light. He looks like the proverbial trusted, likely somewhat overpaid assistant. The two polite goons that did the pickup have long since evaporated.

"Let's get started. I have set aside some time to listen to your story. Who are you, and why are you here?".

Passing the Buck

At eleven in the morning, most hotels are past the check-out rush, with hours before the new guests arrive to check in.

The man carrying a manila envelope takes a careful look around the lobby of the La Fonda Hotel, perhaps the most tradition-laden hotel in Santa Fe. The kind of look one tends to cast if searching for a contact or checking for surveillance. Or if one is lost. This guy is neither a courier, for that he is way overdressed, nor does he look lost. He waits patiently until the agent at the desk looks up, quickly putting on a fake smile and then asks, "How can I help you, sir?"

"Hi. I'd like to drop off this envelope for Todd Dupree."

A substantial-sized envelope changes hand. The clerk has no idea of its content.

The clerk gives off no signal that he has understood the request and is typing away. In cases like that, the smartass response would be to request that he print out the first chapter as soon as it is finished— however, that would draw attention to the visitor, and drawing attention is the last thing this visitor desires. The search takes a few seconds.

"Mister Dupree has not checked in yet. I'll be delighted to hold the envelope for him, however." The envelope changes hands, and it disappears in some invisible drawer.

This is why it's done

Mister Dupree's team met as a group the first time weeks ago in a hotel suite in Manhattan. Some knew each other from earlier life, some not at all. The team was initially divided into a Research Planning and Design Group and into what is being referred to euphemistically as an Operations Team. All are smart, in different ways, however. The Action boys, the Operations Team, with just one exception, had been Blackwater private security people and worked in Iraq and Afghanistan. All the ex-Blackwater boys had slipped past a criminal indictment by the skin of their teeth for what the CSI investigators referred to as excessive force. Meaning they wasted civilians. Their attitude did not improve much after they had been fired because of the uproar the CSI investigation created.

Todd Dupree, a.k.a Morales, had done his homework and established through fairly intensive digging that all ex-Blackwater team members had the same profile and the same underlying problem finding and keeping gainful employment. Most had menial jobs in retail, and some in warehouse security for the simple reason that pre-employment checks of the most superficial kind revealed their checkered past. Their current job description vaguely described their duties in such a way that it was painfully clear that their mission was to intimidate customers and staff. At the end of the first few months, the effectiveness of such an approach became evident when the stores got around to measuring the loss rate. Theft by customers stealing from the shelves of the store and the losses from the warehouse inventory committed by staff were way down. Hiring tough guys works.

The Planners are a totally different story. Here brawn is replaced with brains. In this group, their willingness to accept the risks associated with violence is minimal. Their forte is revealed when sharp, out-of-the-box thinking is required. During the planning phase, the planner's responsibility is to draw up a plan of action, assign budgets, quantify risks, and rewards. The planned project, in most ways, is just another potential business venture. Back at the initial meeting, Todd outlined the objective in very superficial terms, to give those invited an option to decide their level of interest and whether to stay or leave. All they know is that the project involved stealing something mighty valuable and selling it to the highest bidder. Todd deftly implied that it might be a piece of art. And the more creative therefore assumed that art was a euphemism for bearer shares.

Funding for the project came from Todd's circle of fat cat friends, many of whom dabbled in the drug trafficking business. The level at which these guys are engaged in the drug business makes them neither a drug lord a la El Chapo, nor do they stand at street corners peddling crack cocaine. Not a manufacturer, nor a smuggler, nor a retail vendor but rather a wholesale distributor. A major commitment from Gonzales finally provided the bulk of the funding. The illicit drug business has the same structure as any high-margin commodity product distribution channel. And it's all cash. Cash that needs to be laundered. It is that business where Todd became the sophisticated, suave businessman he now mimics. He sees himself as cool. A cool Dude with a substantial number of skeletons in his closet.

This is how it's done

The largest hotel in Santa Fe that offers privacy is the Eldorado. Often used to put up convention attendees, it offers meeting rooms, a business center, and a most convenient location in the center of the old town. A place where, given the proper appearance, anyone can blend in.

The reservation for the group that rented the Taos suite claimed to be in the fashion retail business. Of course, that claim is far from the truth. The room was swept for bugs, and the curtains have been drawn, all notepaper in front of the participants has discreetly been marked so as to reveal the owner if any record from this get-together is ever leaked. Todd is confident that this is one conservative group with a keen sense of tradecraft.

Todd waits patiently for everyone to find their seats.

"Gentlemen, welcome. I will skip introductions until we have settled the first order of business. If anyone has decided to forgo this opportunity, please say so now." No one even bats an eyelash. Anyone lacking the time or the inclination would not have shown up in the first place.

"Again—let me emphasize that this is the last time any of you have a chance to leave. Once you are in, that option no longer exists. As we proceed you will realize why." While the words are friendly and business-like, it is clear to all in the room that what was said is a threat. And all present know that threats made by a drug distributor have teeth. Typically, although this remains unsaid, leaving the project once the plan has been revealed, will involve a bucket of concrete for the feet of the offender to be slipped into and the combination thereof to be tossed overboard from a boat at sea.

"No one. Fabulous." He pauses, scans the group. "Let me outline why we have gathered here in broad terms. Let me present you with an overview of the business opportunity."

Todd's jacket comes off, and he stands up in front of a whiteboard. Just another business meeting.

"What is the most valuable commodity in the world at his moment in time? Intelligence? Stamps? Drugs? Real estate? Art? Weapons? Diamonds?"

Again, total silence since the question was meant rhetorically.

"The correct answer is weapons. Weapons of mass destruction are the most valuable commodity for one simple reason: hostile nation-states and terrorist organizations have a great deal of incentive to procure such devices. Those states that have WMDs will jump through almost any kind of hoop to keep them away from anyone else who is not so equipped at this time. Those states and those terrorist organizations that do not have access to WMD will equally make every conceivable effort to procure such gizmos."

Todd flicks his pen at the group, checking their level of attention.

"What qualifies as a WMD? Anything that kills a lot of people efficiently." The minds of those in attendance are spinning. Biowarfare would be an option. Botulinus toxin. Plague. Anthrax. Ebola. Even chemical weapons like Sarin gas.

To be an effective threat, it is essential that everyone aware of such weapons clearly understands the implications of unlawful ownership.

Todd feels an urge to come to the point. "Everyone present please realize that monetary value is relative and mostly depends on who the buyer is likely to be. Also: if the threat is significant enough, the monetary value is unlimited. Unlimited."

Todd repeats himself. Slowly. Deliberately. Menacingly. "The correct answer is nuclear weapons. Why? Because Hiroshima and Nagasaki, by today's standards mere firecrackers, as well as Chernobyl, Three Mile Island, the Tsunami in Japan, and other nuclear near-catastrophes have taught us their potential. Everyone understands."

As a disciplined group, all are expected to hold their tongues until invited to pose questions or interject comments. Everyone will end up violating this rule.

Todd continues in the same measured tone. What the military likes to call command attitude is clearly on display.

"A nuclear weapon is extremely difficult to build. And extremely expensive. And while some aspects of design, testing and production can be camouflaged, others cannot. Let's start with the fissionable fuel, either Uranium 235 or Plutonium 239. While the production methods are vastly different, both involve building large, industrial facilities that consume vast amounts of power and coolant, and are therefore difficult and expensive to hide. Remember that satellites can determine that an object was recently placed outside if it is the size of a small garbage can or bigger."

He continues with, "Should such production succeed, your terrorist's problems are just starting. PU239 is extremely toxic and very, very difficult to achieve fission with—when the chain reaction sets in. For U235, there is an easier way to make it go boom. The easier way, however, leads to a huge and heavy weapon that's difficult to deliver on a target. Especially if you have to smuggle it into a foreign country that may or may not be alert and suspicious."

To lighten the tone a bit, he explains that there are rumors about the Russian's ability to build a device small enough to fit in a suitcase. The punch line is that ". . . however, the Russians don't know how to build a suitcase."

He realizes that he is going off topic and waves his hand. "Alas, I digress. Stealing a complete, industrially-produced weapon, opens a whole new can of worms. First of all, such devices are stored in bunkers and are heavily protected. All nations that operate a nuclear deterrent are extremely paranoid about the possibility of theft, either by external forces or through an inside job. Let's for the moment assume that this can be done. To make use of a heisted, ready-for-deployment nuclear device, a whole slew of security measures must be defeated. The first one on the list is a component called PAL, short for Permissive Action Link. This component manages every aspect of the detonation cycle, from arming to detonation. It also checks if all conditions that are required for detonation are being met. One such condition is the entry of a complex code sequence. Where does this code originate? In the White House on the order of the President. If the wrong code is entered or an attempt is made to open a completed weapon, this will trigger a non-fission explosion. This will destroy the weapon, making the plutonium or uranium useless. Sitting on the device and drilling holes through the shell will not help much either. And it will kill the guy with the power-drill. The PAL is hidden deep inside the weapon. And by the way: The device's casing is a capacitor that senses penetration."

Todd is waiting for a second to deliver his best punch line yet.

"Bypassing a PAL should be, as one weapons designer graphically put it, about as complex as performing a tonsillectomy while entering the patient from the wrong end."

The joke is rewarded with a brief, classy, mutual burst of laughter.

"Back to stealing a weapon: complete weapons, we learn, are not complete. The electronic control system for targeting, arming, and delivering a nuclear weapon is divided into separate subsystems. For example, a hypothetical nuclear bomb, hanging below the wing of a fighter jet or placed on top of a rocket needs to be delivered via a vehicle-specific, weapon-specific black box that doesn't come with the weapon. That comes with the plane or the ICBM."

He looks around and asks, "Everybody still with us?"

"Next. The transportation logistics of nuclear weapons recognize that it is during transport between bases, storage, and maintenance that a complete weapon is most vulnerable, more so than in storage. Moving nukes around, being done all the time, is the job of OST, Office of Secure Transportation, part of DOE—the Department of Energy. These boys operate the Transportation Control Center, TEC, at Kirtland Air Force Base in Albuquerque. And that organization dispatches a fleet of trucks called 'Safeguard Transporters.'"

Baffled faces everywhere. "So, the Pentagon runs a trucking business?"

"These are modern trailers we cannot recognize as being anything special on the interstate. But they are loaded with a bunch of nasty tricks, like liquid foam capable of turning solid in seconds that can be called upon to fill the entire—the entire trailer—encasing the weapon. Let's not forget the ordinary-looking chase vehicles, driving in front of and behind the Transporter. A simple, slightly aging, slightly dented dark green Chevy Suburban might hide armed guards behind a very dark window tint. Guards willing and equipped to follow shoot-to-kill orders."

Todd is looking at Mike to determine how his prose sinks in with his audience. Speed it up a bit, Mike signals with a rolling motion of his index finger.

"Let me give you a Nuclear Physics 101 primer. This is to make the plot thicken, as they say. Ok, so, if stealing a complete weapon is not a promising approach, stealing the part that is hardest to produce, namely the fuel, shows more promise. A modern nuclear weapon is a multistage fission-fusion-fission thermonuclear device with a variable yield up to a megaton of TNT. As in five hundred thousand tons to a million tons. Stealing a Pit, merely part of a weapon, removes the most expensive and difficult to keep secret step for building a garage-built weapon, still requiring a lot of bits and pieces that are tricky to acquire or manufacture. The Pit is the first stage trigger or fuse: it's essentially a hollow egg-shaped sphere that will be compressed by a two-point-initiated conventional explosive charge. You don't have to remember this—it's not on the test. The explosive is conventional, the shape of the charge is very unconventional and, again, tricky to design. Compressing the Pit changes the geometry from sub-critical to super-critical in microseconds. The explosion shock wave travels at seven miles per second. In older generation weapons, these Pits were the size of a grapefruit. Modern Pits are maybe two to three inches in diameter, weighing a mere 3 kilograms. The yield of the first stage is a fraction of the completed thermonuclear weapon, but let us remember that a few kiloton yield will level a whole city block with ease. Not useful for war but plenty of bang for terrorism."

Todd decides that it might be time for a lunch break. He knows that unless he approaches the point where the plot thickens, as they say, no one will end up eating and that the group will be confronted with an irresistible desire to engage in heated critique about what they heard. Then again, everybody might get too hungry at too late a stage of the afternoon, so he decides to go for raw suspense and proceed with lunch. The fringe benefits of lunch right now also allows for checking if what was said was also understood.

The Plot Thickens

After lunch and a brief group trip to the bathroom, Todd's lecture continues.

"The objective: steal one complete Pit from LANL, either before or after having gone through the refurbishment and re-manufacturing process. It is not necessary that what's stolen will ever become a nuclear weapon. The threat alone is enough to make the buyer cough up fabulous amounts of cash. This will require a significant investment in men, material, and time. All efforts before the actual heist obviously must remain undetected. The research for this project is already well underway. More on that later. Once the heist has been completed, the fact that the U.S. has a Broken Arrow situation will become painfully obvious to the authorities. We must assume that at some point, the identity of some or all involved will be discovered. Not to worry, we have a plan for that as well."

A hand that had gone up, mid-sentence, is being withdrawn. The time for asking about the time after the raid has not come yet.

"Once the device is in our hands, an offer will be leaked to anyone interested. The most efficient path for that leak is likely to pass through those who supply weapons and munitions to rogue governments or terrorist organizations. Or those known to recruit fighters for ISIS. The purpose of these offers is simply to raise the price through bidding. The bid's winner would ideally be the U.S. government, who will desperately want to get their property back. Why target the government? The U.S. treasury has tons upon tons of small, used, non-sequential dollar bills that had been confiscated from the drug trade. Millions upon millions. Enough Mexican shoreline living, drowning in girls and booze for everyone."

For a brief moment, just about all present are unable to suppress a brief smile in anticipation of such a time.

Todd continues. "How do we gain access to a Pit? While the Pits are within the secure perimeter of the Lab, LANL will rely mostly on the overall security of the Lab. However, once the stuff is out on the road, incoming or outgoing, which on the one hand seems to make things easier for a heist, in general, the violence needed to succeed is deemed counterproductive. Such an approach will make a lot of noise, smoke—and there'd be bloodshed— and it would draw immediate public attention to the fact that something is wrong. And those charged with countermeasures will have no other distractions. So, the preferred method of getting close to a nuclear Pit is to create chaos inside or near the perimeter of the Lab as a distraction. Preferably chaos that, while having defenses prepared and ready in a drawer, will require the Lab to adapt and come up with a spontaneous response that seems smart, but whose effectiveness is unproven. A forest fire will do just fine for such a purpose."

Todd manages to share his pride for the concept with the Planners by nodding in their direction.

"The plan, therefore, will rely on a tactically placed wildfire near the perimeter of the Lab. A wildfire in that area will prompt the influx of hundreds of firefighters, ranging from the Lab's own, to the local community fire department, to all kinds of corporate, communal, and federal firefighters. Some from the Federal Forest service. None in identical uniforms or equipment. At some point, safety will supersede security. That's the moment we are waiting for. We will have to catch one or more of the Pits during the emergency response that will be improvised during the reaction to the fire. A bunch of volunteer firefighters showing up when such guys are most desperately needed will receive limited scrutiny. The 'Show me your papers' command is not the first thing to come to mind if the back of your pants are on fire."

Todd tries to draw his audience into a dialogue. "How do you start a forest fire? And who knows how to do that? It may seem ludicrous, but most forest fires are set by the very people charged with fighting such fires. How is that done? A fire-starter dispenser spits out table-tennis sized balls filled with potassium permanganate. Just before the balls are ejected from a helicopter's onboard dispenser, a small amount of glycerin is injected into the object. A chemical reaction between the two agents, meeting the first time, will a few seconds later have generated enough heat to make the sphere burst into flames as it falls to the ground. Bingo: instant forest fire. This technique is used to create firebreaks by back-burning for removing fuel for future forest fires. Often thousands of such balls are dropped from a slow-flying helicopter at the rate of one or two per second. Many magicians use that same chemistry to make things burst into flames by magic wand."

A hand goes up, and this one does not come down. "Do we have information about how fast such a fire can spread? The plan will fail if the fire's spread is brought under control quickly."

One of the planners coughs to attract attention and responds. "A helicopter will be dispensing fire starters traveling a low altitude at maybe 30 knots. In one minute, that's 2600 feet, dispensing between 60 and 150 flaming balls, each maybe 25 to 50 feet apart. We observed fire drills at the Lab, and we guess that it takes ten minutes for them to launch a mission. The first one to arrive will be a command vehicle that has no role other than observing and reporting. In ten minutes, that aircraft has traveled five miles, leaving behind one hell of a fire."

Moderately doubtful looks are met with a knowing stare: the planner is confident and proud of his data.

"The device is called, of all things, AIDS, a machine officially known as an Aerial Ignition Device. What the final S stands for, no one knows."

The hand attached to the questioner goes up again. "They will know that we are coming."

Our planning genius has an answer, of course. "Yep, they will. We, on the other hand, will make sure that they are looking in the wrong spot, because there will be two fires. A small one at the gate we target, a large one a mile in the wrong direction."

Another break. Those not used to endless meetings really need a break. Just about everybody stands up, stretching their legs for a few minutes, then it's back to work.

The meeting is called to order. A raised hand and a discrete cough from Mike gradually silences the chatter. Todd ponders the purpose of Mike's unsolicited initiative.

Could it be that he is elbowing his way to take over the command spot?

"Everybody set? Okay." Todd stares at Mike, "Next, we need to look at the timetable and then dish out procurement assignments. For the time being, let's operate under the premise that there will be eight of us on the actual mission and six of us in the planning and design group. So, when obtaining goodies for all members, buy twenty units of whatever including the spares, for Operations buy twelve and for Planning, buy eight."

Looking around, Todd's finger seeks out someone non-descript at the back and attracts his attention. "No need to take notes: I have handouts on the table at the door. First, we need cash for everyone. Now, remember that cash is untraceable, but often not accepted for purchases that are, say larger than one hundred bucks. For those purchases, let us purchase anonymous, pre-paid gift debit cards. Put two grand five hundred on each. We'll need multiple pre-paid burner phones for everybody. Do not activate these till you are given the word. The cash is already here. Everyone gets an envelope with five grand." Todd is mighty proud of the idea of borrowing and laundering money from one crime to finance the next crime.

Another member of the planning group gets the job of finding handcuffs, Tasers, and pepper spray. Guns and ammo came from Todd's past business relationships; all with milled off serial numbers, some obtained at gun shows, some from crooked dealers that fiddle inventory accounting to supply weapons to the cartels south of the border.

"A civilian Bell Huey, a Bambi bucket and a Dragon Firestarter, the AIDS machine, officially known as an Aerial Ignition Device we leased from a broker, claiming that someone in our office has submitted a bid to work fires for the Forest Service. The lease's first three-month estimates have already been paid. Fuel will get billed to an account that has been in use for years by now." Someone wants to know how that miracle was accomplished. Todd is proud to show off the meticulous plotting that has gone into the project. "Easy, my friend. We bought a small outfit that had run out of funds, easy to locate in the general aviation business, and we paid up all their outstanding liabilities. Like insurance, some Bell parts that we could not send back, the hangar rent, and of course, the outstanding fuel invoice. There is nothing left to alert anyone."

Todd introduces the next topic. The small, simple to obtain and hard to trace procurement items are now off the table, so the time has come to turn the attention to ground transportation. "We will need a whole fleet of ground transportation vehicles. Some we steal right before the heist; replacement license plates will be lifted a day before from cars parked at the Dallas airport. Let's pick cars that look like they have been parked there for a while. Even if the owner gets back before the operation is executed, the fact that the plates are missing might not become obvious right away. Out of state plates also makes it harder for any curious cop to check the registration. So, the policy is as follows: cars that we will use for an extended period of time, we shall purchase from private individuals, pay cash and then hold off sending in the title paperwork; the public records, therefore, will still show the vehicle registered to the seller. These cars better be older, popular models such as Honda Elements—those boxy things specifically designed for ugly kindergarten teachers. Regardless of model, make sure that they are non-descript cars without OnStar or other built-in communications gear, the kind that calls 911 when the airbags deploy. We also need one more motor home. One, we park at Lake Cochiti, and that one will later be parked near Albuquerque airport as the outbound staging vehicle where we change into new clothes, grab our goodies, and disappear into the sunset. Tickets on shuttle buses from Albuquerque to Chihuahua are on order for us. No gringos ever use these buses. We may change our escape plans yet, but for the moment this is the planned way out of the country for those of us still here by then."

But there is more.

"The other camper will become our communications and command center. That one will go to the Los Alamos campground, complete with pre-recorded noises of a dog, acting as a decoy or distraction. We had it there already for a few hours to make sure all our needs are catered for. And that's where we had a close call, but that's also been taken care of." There is no obvious advantage to divulge the outcome of Chris's suspicion and her demise.

Todd's care in his selective disclosure of the plan's details is admirable.

"We will need three Zodiacs, inflatable boats, powered by both gasoline and by battery. Specifications to be found in the handout. Wetsuits must be purchased. Rock climbing gear needs to be added to the list."

"Next, this is a bit trickier," he explains, "we will need two different, but related challenges addressed. First, we need a Draisine. What in the world is a Draisine, one might ask?" He continues, "A Draisine is a small, motorized vehicle that runs on railroad tracks. They are used by track maintenance crews to move men, material, and tools between the maintenance shop and the work location. The handout explains what make and model we are shopping for. Make it a lease or a purchase; do NOT acquire by theft. Do this ASAP. We need to make modifications, see the handout for that as well. Second, we need one of the researchers to make a table of train movement on the rail line between Albuquerque and Lamy, in either direction. When they depart, where and when they stop. The works. Passenger trains, freight, and Railrunner shuttle. Make it precise, seven-twenty-four. May and June only. And we need this verified through observation. Someone is going to sit near the track to check the table. More than once."

73

A guy called Jose is called to the front and introduced as the drone pilot. He is Hispanic, short, scar-faced, and carries impeccable qualifications flying surveillance drones for the Sinaloa cartel out of Los Mochis. It was Jose who had climbed the ravine from the Rio Grande up to the tree to install the game camera outside TA-55.

"Jose, please explain how drones will be used in this operation."

Jose's Hispanic accent makes it difficult to follow, but everyone figures out that the plan is to fly small camera drones and park these in the treetops near the gate. Some of the questions that follow clearly piss off both Todd and Jose. Questions about the radar cross-section of a small drone, made mostly of non-metallic components. "We did some tests at the other end of the restricted airspace that covers the Lab, and we have established that drone penetration will not alert the controller, sitting in the Los Angeles Center, remotely monitoring airspace violations. He's looking for objects with at least one hundred times more radar cross-section than a plastic drone. The drone imagery will allow the command center to pick the exact time when each segment of this operation will be triggered via radio." Todd points out by whom, leaving no room for speculation or inviting discourse.

Harry at Home

I distinctly remember learning quickly that running a small aviation charter business requires a facility on the grounds of the base airport for simple, practical reasons. The airport is where all the records are kept, where the main listed phone line rings and then gets forwarded to my cellphone. Customers with Real Money have knowledge of my cell number. And this is where a sofa awaits a weary pilot at the end of a long flight.

It turned out that the most efficient, cost-effective solution to my office space requirements was an aging but functional camper sitting up against the outside wall of the hangar. I become the proud owner when a small-time rancher could not pay my bill that he accrued for me flying rolls of barbed wire. Now it sits on a couple of cement blocks in lieu of the deflated tires.

As I approach the door to my professional abode, I hear faint noise that I know must come from my faithful dog climbing off the sofa, strictly off-limits while I am inside. The door is locked with a keypad, and as soon as I start pressing the required keystrokes, I can hear Zorro, my three-year-old German Sheppard, sniffing at the door resolving the friend versus foe question. The door opens, and before I can step inside, my hand gets a quick, silent lick.

Sometimes I am gone for most of the day, leaving the dog behind in the climate-controlled camper. In the maintenance facility—their office is on the other side of the hangar—I found a kind soul, a short, chubby receptionist who's in love with Zorro and me. She carefully keeps track of the dog's needs and takes him out when a walk comes due. The dog rewards her for her affection. I don't.

When one Googles Zorro, one learns that ". . . Zorro, a fictional character, was created in 1919 by writer Johnston McCulley. The masked, sword-wielding vigilante defends the poor and victimized against the forces of injustice" —thus, it's a proper name for my dog. Sort of a Hispanic canine Robin Hood. Initially, I wanted a Great Dane, but I thought I might not be able to resist naming him Hamlet, a move that would have, deservedly so, earned me the reputation of a snob.

While I really appreciate the convenience of having an on-airport office, that fact also implies a never-ending struggle to keep work-related papers, calendars, and all sorts of radio gear in the right place. A simple trick seems to have solved most of my troubles with forgetfulness: both at home and at the airport I have a tray that was initially intended to carry drinks with little umbrellas and that now serves as the temporary container to collect sunglasses, keys, my cellphone and other objects prone to be left behind. Zorro sits at the bottom of the bookshelf with that tray, anticipating the moment all its contents wander back to my pockets as the most surefire way for the animal to determine that our departure is imminent. Zorro is well aware of my work habits and has learned to blend in smoothly, anticipating with amazing skill when the time has come to climb into an aging Chevy Avalanche for the ride home. And home is where a quick walk, an urgent pee, a snack, and a bowl of fresh water will be consumed in what seems to be mere seconds. Zorro will have the same.

My current residence is predictably on the wrong side of the tracks. Now, Santa Fe has housing for Everyone. Las Campanas, an upscale golf development has mansions that would be the envy of Malibu. My place is on Agua Fria, far enough south so that most neighbors have the seemingly obligatory collection of cars in various stages of disrepair. It's reasonably safe, compared to Albuquerque, a city with many times the daily murder rate of Sweden. The safety here is mostly the result of firefighters, and later cops, who started buying up and renovating some of the trashier single-family homes. With these families came some form of order solely because these guys only put up with a limited amount of bullshit.

In general, the local demographics are as expected: about half are Hispanic, a third are Anglos, a few blacks, one Indian family. No Asians. No Europeans. Mostly, surprisingly, blue-collar but more often than not liberal, their political views clearly on display through years-old bumper stickers praising Obama. My fading "Jon Stewart for President" sticker blends in beautifully.

Our city has no industry, so most employment is coming out of government, construction, and tourism. Many of the residents are here legally. Many are not. The ones here illegally are typically the cream of the crop if you are looking for help of some sort: illegals will make every attempt to legitimize themselves by being honest and hard working. And they will really try to keep their Anglo employer from getting pissed off since ICE's deportation officers are a mere phone call away.

For me, the real upside is the place's proximity to the airport. Not on any instrument approach. KSAF essentially has few night arrivals and departures. Actually, I am personally responsible for about half the night noise coming off the airport.

My place is on a half-acre lot. It's a rental. Looks like Adobe, the traditional building material of the Southwest, but it is built by Post and Beam—even rarer now in these latitudes. The house is in beautiful shape. The owner is a dentist who used to live there when new in town. He did some major renovations and I did, as the first rental tenant, some minor enhancements. Twelve-hundred square feet for one person and one dog turned out to be acceptable. I have been here for six years now. The furnishings are sparse and run the gamut from beanbags to Louis XV replicas. Most of it has been sourced at Ikea with no interior decorator taking responsibility for the lack of a consistent style. My cleaning lady, originally from Chihuahua like so many, can claim responsibility for the near orderly appearance of the inside; she is smart enough to stay out of the garage. She does, however, hide the stuff that clutters up the home in places where such items traditionally reside in a Mexican's home. And these hiding places can be a bitch to find. She sees this as a sport, and I see it as an anti-aging brain exercise.

Yet twelve-hundred square feet, plus a stuffed two-car garage, isn't a lot of extra space. The first garage spot is for the Avalanche. The other place is occupied with a vintage Jaguar Xk120, currently—meaning it's been slowly and intermittently worked on for five years—under refurbishment. In order not to be reminded that the project needs work, it is covered with a dusty silver plastic cover.

A chicken pot pie, frozen and oven-ready, will emerge shortly from the microwave. I am hungry—no reason to waste time and effort cooking for one hungry Harry.

Dinner with an Old Buddy

Ian Larson is a friend, a Dirty Harry type friend, the type of man that in any self-respecting B-movie will be cast as The Sympathetic Villain.

He says and does all the things that I cannot do or say. We often think the same, however.

He is anti-establishment, deep down a bit of a racist. He is profoundly immoral and willing to break the law. Anti-authoritarian. A very smart and quick on his feet slob. It has been said that a faint smell of sulfur trails him.

He drives an old Toyota truck with a camper shell in the back. His rear windows are covered with stickers to prove that he has been to Mexico, Alaska, Canada, Guatemala, Honduras, El Salvador, and for that reason, he cannot see out the back.

He chases skirts relentlessly, often with admirable success. Ian subscribes to the catch-and-release method.

He dresses for events worthy of such effort like Sam Elliot: lengthy grey hair, jeans, boots, and a substantial mustache. Same basso profundo voice as well, yet he resists the temptation to go for the Awww Shucks accent of aging aviators—the most beautiful example of that accent coming from Chuck Yeager. Ian used to fly for a living. Fixed-wing, not Helicopters; I occasionally remind him that he flew aircraft anybody can fly.

Every instance where the magic words "Hold my beer and watch this" were uttered, I was with him. We haven't done much of the crazier stuff in a while, but we did a while back. Back when, as Billy Joel so aptly put it, ". . . I wore a younger man's clothes." We rib each other incessantly. He thinks of me as Charlie Harper, and I think of him, if you can ignore the gender adjustment, as Berta (in the same TV series). To round off the description: he has a habit, at his peril, of speaking in fake Native American English. As in "Me Injun, white man speaks with forked tongue."

I felt a need to disclose to him what was on my mind.

We planned to have dinner at Maria's Mexican Kitchen. I made a reservation a day or so back for seven. The length of the queue for tonight, when I approached the receptionist, is a clear indication that planning is often rewarded here. On a Friday night, the place looks much like the Bar Scene in Star Wars, anything from sizable Mexican families to fake Texans wearing Birkenstock sandals with spurs. Okay, I made that up.

The barkeeper fixes me one of his fabulous Margaritas. I am a bit early, so I order the first drink to tie me over till Ian shows up. I pay careful attention to the barkeeper's expertise yet one more time, and this reveals the trick that's been used here since 1945 to achieve such glory: stick with a lot of really good quality booze and freshly squeezed lemon juice.

I am facing away from the entrance. I can smell the beer and the most recent cigar on his breath as Ian approaches me from behind. He is out of breath, just having run the gauntlet across Cordova Street from a shopping mall parking lot. We have been friends for quite a while, so we dispense with formalities. A fist bump replaces the traditional handshake or the bear hug that seems to be *en vogue*.

"Been up to no good?" he inquires.

"Nope. Great day. A bit boring. I had a long photoshoot up the river. Amateurs. Anything to keep the rotors spinning."

Ian is familiar with my staccato style of speaking when I am with those who know me well.

The waiter approaches. Water glasses are being waved away, since water, by this duo at least, is considered mere clutter on the table.

"The blue corn enchiladas with Carne Adovado, red chili, and another Horny Toad, salt, rocks, would hit the spot. And bring some Sopapillas, enough for both of us." The waiter reads back the order. His questioning look at Ian elicits a one-word response. "Same." Efficiency can be wonderful.

Ian has a checkered past. He started out as a soldier, the path to an education for many of those with impoverished parents. Even many years ago, a college education, the key to success, regardless of how you measure success, was unavailable to those who grew up in a trailer park. Ian made it, despite a semi-retired hooker as a mother and a drunk as an absentee father. That's how cynics are bred, and he indeed is a bit of a cynic. That's part of what bonds us.

Now he works odd jobs in construction, a field of endeavor populated with gifted amateurs going for a quick buck. That fact alone might well be the cause of the never-ending maintenance issues many recent American homeowners get to experience. I like him and trust his work, despite a ceaselessly leaking showerhead in my place that he hadn't been able to fix yet. I fastidiously decline to do home maintenance myself.

As the evening crowd shuffles in, Ian's eye wanders effortlessly between arriving and departing women of all ages. When he approves of a new-arrival, a typical comment from him would be, "Have her washed and brought to my chambers."

In the middle of chewing on chunks of the delicious pork, he starts with, "I ran into an old enemy from a few years back, real hard-ass . . ." He stops mid-sentence. He saw my face.

I stare at him. Generally, I don't make it my business to teach social manners to others; I have enough on my hands handling my own. While I am neither a prude nor a snob—I can be condescending towards the uncultured—talking while eating drives me nuts. I am also tired of showing folks with which fork to eat the soup. He gulps down both the pork and his truncated story.

The Margaritas arrive, filled to the rim, so the gentlest of nods replaces any and all riskier maneuvers. "Salud." "Na zdorovie." Some traditions must remain sacred.

I concluded that the time had come to approach the next question gingerly. "And what, pray tell, have you been up to this fine day?"

"I bought beads for my squaw." Ian has a girlfriend. Actually, it's more an affair with a married woman. I speculate about the carat weight of the trinket Ian acquired, him being pretty cheap. Her husband sits in a prison somewhere on the East Coast, a geographically undesirable situation. She is not Native American by any stretch of the imagination. She was the result of a one-night stand between a pretty French women living in Tahiti and a German ship officer. Natalie is forty-two, exotic, has European facial features, honey-colored skin, pitch-black hair, and, this is what Ian is attracted to, a wild streak. I fondly remember a threesome between us in a hot tub; both were pretty mellow from smoking pot. I don't touch the stuff, but I am looking forward to the day when I no longer fly. Cannabis consumption is frowned upon by the FAA, a pilot's peers and his passengers. Other than Natalie, Ian is committed to the never-ending pursuit of female companionship.

While we wait for the drinks to arrive, I see the camera crew from this morning being led to a table in the next room. They chat as they walk by, and I remain unnoticed, which is just fine—after a long day on a small island, we have not much to say that hasn't been said already. In addition to the three this morning, a new face has joined them. He looks ex-military, he is a touch older, significantly less buff, maybe he has been flying a desk for a while. Overall, the group's appearance has been cleaned up a bit, and the body language between the ground members indicates the pecking order—if this is not a social gathering, then the new guy is the boss. As they are sitting down, all are still wearing sunglasses that are being packed away in eyeglass cases or exchanged with reading glasses. Since I am facing away from their partially hidden table down some stairs, my view of that table is reflected by a mirror that I am facing. Their orders arrive—mostly drinks and appetizers, making the meal short enough to suggest more plans for the evening. A little later, while we are mopping up our dinner, the group pays, gets up, and they vanish in a cloud of vapors that smells of Margarita.

And then there is Erin

I am a member of the local Experimental Aircraft Association Group. Homebuilders and all sorts of aviators, ranging from would-be pilot students to old fogies, and pilots way past their prime, hanging around hangars to tell tall lies gather monthly. I am the only one remotely qualified to talk about rotary-wing flight. This month's meeting takes place at Double Eagle Airport in Albuquerque. I hate to drive that far for lukewarm beer and bone-dry hamburgers; I do feel obliged to show up more or less regularly, however. Often, after the meeting formally ends, someone will hang back before going home, to ask questions or brag about their adventures in helicopters.

Most members of this chapter are known to me. But not all. Every other meeting participant and I immediately notice a new face. A woman.

She is blondish, and she has short, practical hair, big, bright brown eyes. No ring. Not wearing comfortable shoes—thus not lesbian. She is wearing very little makeup. No handbag. Mid-thirties? She is toned and tanned. No visible tan lines, therefore not a Nun either. Five feet ten, one hundred and forty pounds. Striking looks. Using a scale of one to six, she is a fabulous eight. In a cocktail dress, possibly a nine. Right now, she's wearing black slacks and a simple white blouse, typical office uniform for a woman intent on climbing the corporate ladder. Every male in the room sucks in his stomach, a trick that only works for a very short period of time, then the belly pops back to its original, less favorable position. I managed five seconds —long enough.

She ends up in the chair next to me. Toward the end of the meeting, when first-time visitors show up and are asked to introduce themselves, she reveals that she has taken glider lessons, went on her first solo, flew for a while, and then dropped out of flying. We chat briefly about her past. My instant assessment is: witty, flirty, determined, assertive, smart. She is dismissive of fools I discover quickly. In most ways, my kind of woman. Ah, hell, in every way, my kind of woman. Males who often share their bed with a German Shepherd, lacking a better alternative, will understand. I am consistently hopeful that one of these days the dog will end up back where he belongs, namely the warm spot on the floor in the living room, freeing up the place on the left side of my king size bed.

Before I get up, she indicates that she'd love to chat. About my favorite topic: flying.

She works as the spokesperson for the local hospital. Erin was a medical student who ran out of money in pursuit of a seemingly elusive academic goal, right after she ran out of money for the glider flying. She is interested in art. She wants to go and learn to fly helicopters. Doesn't cook worth a damn, she claims. Is it possible that her weak spots are exactly my strengths?

"Tell me about flying helicopters," she solicits. I'll be delighted. She jokes that she heard that them things are just waiting to fall out of the sky. My standard response polished to a fine hone will hopefully dazzle her. I give it my best shot.

"Since you have flown gliders, much of what I'll say will apply to rotary wings flight as well. But if I bore you, please stop me, ok?"

Her response is quite cute: "Let it rip."

"Flying fixed wing is a science, flying helicopters is an art. An art is a skill one must acquire and then hone, one that only few are born with a talent for. A skill that is prone to teach you humility while learning." Fond memories of my own student pilot days come back, days when my first attempt at hovering required a football field sized spot somewhere in the back of the airport.

"Flying a helicopter is not without risk. Flying one on a nice clear day at sea level in moderate temperatures and a low takeoff weight is considered well within the capabilities of a freshly minted Helicopter pilot. Doing the same thing on a hot, muggy day at ten thousand feet with a full fuel load and a bunch of impatient passengers or a sizable load of cargo is a different story, one that would call for a seasoned pro."

Her bright, attentive eyes indicate that she is following the plot here. By now, I am about knee-deep into falling in lust.

"You want to do this for fun, or you plan to go commercial?" Flying a helicopter for fun rather than for an income changes the direction that the money will flow. Is she in an income category to support such an expensive habit?

Without pause, she responds that it is way too early for such a decision. I asked because essentially everyone chasing a job as a pilot needs a fair bit of experience in their resume, experience that often, but not always, comes from instructing. Green instructors teaching flying to greener students. I know, it sounds insane.

"Now: if simply flying a chopper is not enough of a challenge, I always recommend instruction—teaching helicopter flying from scratch. It is done all the time, both civilian and military instructors face that challenge daily. Doing instruction, the threat is human, not mechanical. Nor hydraulic or electric. Believe me, the threat is human. The student will try to kill you. If you firmly believe that, thou shalt survive." I point out that in defiance of popular belief, helicopters were not designed and developed to hover or fly backwards. Instead, the intent was to cleanse the gene pool of slow thinkers.

My wisecrack is rewarded with a roll of her eyes, followed by an understanding, warm smile. A plan to transition this conversation into a relationship is slowly forming in my mind.

"Recognition of that wisdom tends to make the instructor grab the controls whenever things start to get out of control. That happens often and quickly. And it will happen before the student even realizes that the situation is deteriorating. So, to the student, who is terrified, but ignorant of his most recent misdeed and likely to choose that particular moment to realize that signing up for helicopter lessons was a mistake, will react with a puzzled look on his face. Implied question: what did I do?"

I inquire if my delivery is meeting her expectations. Her response is "Affirmative."

"The downside of the instructor, way ahead of the student, grabbing the controls any time the student doesn't handle the chopper like a seasoned pro, is of course that the student never learns anything. Learning means making mistakes and seeing the consequences. They are followed by applying corrective measures. Plus saying to oneself, 'That was stupid. I ain't gonna do that again.' Words that will be with a pilot for the rest of her or his flying career. We begin to realize that those instructors willing to accept some risk, and instead of grabbing the controls, roll their eyes in the eternal body language of '.... what the hell are you doing?' will turn out a more competent pilot. It is the same, regardless of what you end up flying."

She nods, appearing to enjoy my monologue. I decide to quicken the pace a bit; if her mind wanders, let it wander towards me.

I continue to explain that helicopters are used for many jobs involving external load, like firefighting, logging, construction, rescues—the list is endless. Flying external loads is a tricky business because the pilot controls or flies the load hanging on a long cable below the chopper. The likely pendulum motion can truly ruin one's day. If you accelerate the aircraft, the load wants to lag behind; if you slow down, the load will end up way out in front of the chopper. One of the greater thrills in piloting a helicopter is to get an external load to swing. That will end in a quick disconnect of the load —and a miserable retrieval from wherever it landed.

"Medevac, newscasting about traffic and police activities and movie camera aerial shots tend to restrict the helicopter, once so equipped, to that specialty since to reconfigure the aircraft between different types of usage may not be economically feasible." I pause. Not the time to overdo, time to set up The Kill.

"You interested in some stick time?" The time to gingerly elicit a minor commitment from her has come. I figure that no aviator can resist getting his or her hands on the controls of some new type of aircraft for the first time.

Her eyes light up. "Seriously?" Seriously.

A date, time, and the location are set. I steer the timing towards the late afternoon. The wrong time for flying—the sun will be in our eyes —the right time for a smooth transition to a joint dinner? I say to myself that the time has come to make this one count.

As a parting gift I get what could be referred to as a hug, not close enough and way too short by any means, yet just good enough to make the many observers jealous.

It is a week later by now and she is right on time for her lesson. No wonder: I charmed the socks off her last Tuesday when I promised to show her how to fly a helicopter. I don't do such introductions very often for simple economic reasons. Jet fuel alone is two hundred and fifty dollars per hour when the engine is running, component reserves add another two hundred and fifty, making pro bono flights the high price equivalent of a barkeeper drinking his own booze. Her car slows to a full stop in front of my home; I see mostly shiny white teeth through the windshield, and through the open window I hear her say, "Hi. Great day for flying. I am all excited. You have no idea how much I appreciate your generosity." Baby, hold that thought, there will be a time and a place when you will have an opportunity to express your gratitude. As I climb into her sweet, clean, uncluttered BMW, I hear myself say, "Erin, nice of you to pick me up. Will you drop me off back here when we are done?" The intention is, of course, to create an ample supply of such opportunities. I must keep reminding myself to be patient. Down boy, down.

"I left the bird fueled, with the pre-flight done on the ramp. Both sticks are in." She's wearing jeans and a tank top with the appropriate amount of cleavage that reveals what I suspected, yet what remained concealed by the blouse she wore when we last met.

I intend to make good use of the ten-minute drive to the airport and start out explaining what I planned for her first flight in a helicopter. "Santa Fe is a bit too busy to take the first hop, so I'll take off, and you fly us to Española. No traffic there, and they have a huge ramp where no one ever parks. The whole airport is a total waste of time and Indian casino money. Those comedians thought that the millionaires would fly their Citations to this shithole to come and gamble when with just a few gallons more, they can go to Las Vegas."

She seems surprised, but not anxious about the thought of taking the controls within minutes of taking off. That didn't comply with the rumors she hears about helicopters.

Readily available anecdotes about engine failures prompt her to ask "What happens if the engine quits?" and I respond with "we glide to a gentle landing." Actually, autorotations to a landing share many similarities with behind-the-glass painting: all steps in the process have to be done right the first time.

"Your look tells me that this seems a bit too quick for your taste? Do not worry, flying a helicopter straight and level is a piece of cake for a glider pilot." This might not be the time to tell her about the terrors a greenhorn faces when trying to hover the first time. I was watching her drive, and experience tells me that she'll be fine on that first leg. I am holding my judgment regarding hovering.

She parks smoothly and without hesitation in a tight spot outside the terminal. As I walk to the door that leads to the ramp, I sense that all inside are checking her out.

There is but one Long Ranger sitting out quite a long walk away. As we get closer, the time has come for a few words about the bird.

"We will be light, and we have fuel for ninety minutes, plus thirty reserve. The Long Ranger has a lot of power for that low weight. Twenty minutes will get us to Española, and that will give you a chance to get a feel for her. As I said, piece of cake."

We are there, and I pop her door open. Some leg swinging gets her over the stick and into the seat. I take note that she does not fasten her shoulder belt to be able to lean forward to reach switches should that become necessary. It takes me about fifteen minutes before engine start to go over the controls, skipping most of the switches and many of those instruments that deal with the engine. I do point out some red lines that mark the end of the operating range, and I hint at the consequences of going past those. She understands that punishment for pulling the power past the red line will involve spanking. I get a wink.

Within a few minutes, we are all fired up, the temperatures are all in the green, and we depart northbound. I climb to about one thousand feet above the terrain. Not a word is exchanged; the idea is to let her absorb all the new impressions and map those against what she remembers from her glider flying.

I point out some of the new challenges. "With that huge bubble out front and almost no visual reference to show where the horizon should be, you'll tend to climb or descend. Descending below eight thousand will earn you a reprimand. Don't touch the collective, just point us where you want to go with the cyclic."

She bites her lip; she takes the cyclic control stick with three fingers and says: "My aircraft." Good manners. Nothing happens. We just continue to plow through the sky. After about fifteen seconds, the nose comes down a bit, and we drift ten degrees to the left. Erin is quick to correct. Fast learner. This should be fun.

I point out the town, and she has already noted the runway a bit north of the built-up area. As we follow the main highway, I ask her to lower the collective a touch to seventy percent torque and slow to eighty knots. When we reach pattern altitude, I inform her that I'd like my aircraft back. She concedes, I feel, almost reluctantly. I aim for the ramp and touch down lightly, right in the center of the ramp, and pointing the nose straight into the windsock. The wind blows at less than ten knots.

"How was that?" I inquire. She's all revved up. "Piece of cake, just like you said." Shit-eating grin.

I inquire "Are we having fun yet?" Loads and loads she acknowledges.

I point out that a co-pilot's correct response at this point would be an admiring look and a "Nice landing Sir; I'll buy the first round."

I loosen my seat belt. The time for the more challenging aspects of flying is preceded by some time idling and talking on the ground. My lecture is brief and to the point.

"I shall now teach you how to hover. The easiest control to become familiar with are the pedals; these control the pitch of the tail rotor, whose job it is to offset main rotor torque and give you directional control. They will feel strange, since they do not provide any feedback. All they do is change the pitch of the tail rotor." They are also the least exciting for the instructor because all that can happen is to get the aircraft spinning about its rotor mast axis but in place. Nothing to run into, no chance of hitting the ground.

"For the moment, I will handle cyclic and collective, and you just keep pointing this thing at the windsock, alrighty then?" A chuckle indicates that she's seen Ace Ventura.

I lift off to a low hover and prepare myself to deliver some sarcastic comment, something along the lines of ". . . I meant with the nose, not the tail," but other than some light swinging back and forth, all goes well, and I am deprived of an opportunity to display my finely-honed wit. Time to raise the stakes a bit. "Please turn ninety degrees to the left." Turning takes a mere hint of pedal pressure, but she gets it right and manages to hold it steady.

"Can I have a one-eighty turn to the right?" and at that very moment, all hell breaks loose, and within seconds, we whip around way past the direction I asked for. All I hear is "Oops," and I notice her hand now gripping the cyclic stick with a tight fist and white fingers. I intervene with "Got it," and I set her down on the skids. "Remember, the pedals only." A nod affirms that we are back on the same page.

While I give her a few moments to catch her breath, I ask how far she got into medical school. Not very far, I learn. The time for the delivery of one of my medical wisecracks has arrived: "I am told that in the first two years in the hospital, all a budding physician learns is not to say *oops*." That is, by lack of a response, not considered either funny or appropriate. All my other medical humor deals with one or the other aspects of a colonoscopy. She had planned to go into pediatrics, so I permanently skip those.

We go back in the air, all three feet of it, to practice pedal turns some more. After a quarter-hour, Erin is getting pretty steady at this. Again, we set down on the skids. We chat about her glider flying in an attempt to remind her of her past aerial accomplishments. I aim to build confidence.

My next question, after we have gone over some of the skills she has now picked up, is intended to determine her degree of readiness to conquer the next challenge. "Some more new stuff?" She points out an arriving small single-engine plane; I consider that a positive sign: proof that she is not yet worn out, that she has enough mental capacity left to absorb minor distractions.

"Ok. This time, I will handle the pedals and the collective, you try to stay in one place, right where the yellow taxi-line splits and turns." Unambiguous commands are beneficial at this stage of the training. Once back in the air, she again takes the cyclic between three fingers. It didn't take her long to figure out that the controls on a Bell are mighty sensitive. This is actually the trickiest part of learning to hover, the part that terrifies students. However, this portion of the overall challenge offers the instructor protection because we are a long way away from any obstacle. Limited protection, since some students have a surprising knack for heading straight for the pole with the windsock at a rate that will eat up all the distance in just a few seconds.

It's the next step that offers an opportunity to do real damage, so I keep that for last.

I suggest that the neatest way to stay in one place is to avoid staring down right in front of the bubble, but instead look out a bit further. Well, it turns out that this is either not her best intuitive skill or that she is more worn down than I had concluded. As she wanders around the ramp a bit I make mild cracks along the lines that we are not yet ready for a cross country flight. It takes a while, and over time the back and forth gradually calms down substantially.

We take a brief rest, then try again. It takes longer than I anticipated, but she gets hovering within an acceptable range. I do not comment on the fact that I am pretty pleased with my skills as an instructor while not being overwhelmed by her hovering skills.

Time for the control she hasn't touched yet. "The collective, the lever on your left, can be pulled up or lowered, and this will determine if we climb, hold altitude or descend. The engine senses a need for a power change and will hold RPM with near perfection. It's very sensitive. You'll think you are hanging on a bungy; also, there is an inherent tendency to over-control. Pulling up too aggressive will fire us up in the air, no big deal, but dumping the collective harshly can cause us to hit the ground. Remember, helicopters are not designed to be plowed into a runway on every flight. This is a vehicle for gentlemen, not a 737." Envy and also disdain for those lucky bastards who fly for the airlines need to periodically be expressed. But then, they get told when to visit which bathroom by dispatch in flight operations.

She tries gingerly at first but soon gets the hang of this new challenge, and after a quarter hour, Erin can hold the height of three feet admirably steady.

She lowers the kids until they gently touch the tarmac. More banter, more time to cool down.

She fiddles with the headset to find a more comfortable position while I introduce the next step. "You did well. Proud of you. Next, you try all three controls at the same time, while I step outside for a smoke." I have of course no intention of doing so. She doesn't fall for that old crack, but I notice that she's aware of my feet off the pedals and my hands are away from the controls, in my lap.

"We have about ten minutes left before we have to head back. Ready?" Yep: ready. Kid, nobody is ever ready at this stage.

She is one mighty careful pilot, so the progress is slow. There is the usual slithering around, expletives are expressed, the nose is wandering, and the height is oscillating. It does get better by the minute, however. I don't say much. She sets it down on the skids with a thump this time. Her face is glowing, and her eyes sparkle. I check the time and suggest that ". . . the time to take Daisy to the barn has come."

"Can I take her all the way back to Santa Fe?"

Yes, you can. "Yes, you can."

But the first lesson in a chopper is wearing, and I don't want to risk bursting her confidence, so I choose to deny her the chance to screw things up at the last second. Once we are getting close to Santa Fe, I take over for the last five hundred feet, and I land.

It's time for handing out compliments; as the engine winds down, I lean over as she blows the bangs out of her forehead and I say "Fine job, congrats. Now, in the next lesson we will learn how to use the turn signal," a comment that solicits a "Wise guy" response.

The Pursuit of Erin

Friday is when I like to cook, sometimes for myself (when the dish is known to be prone for failure—as in soufflé), sometimes for friends and neighbors. Tonight, the entertainment system blasting out, on auto-repeat so I can sing along, is "La Malaguena" performed by Placido Domingo. He doesn't really need my help, but I sing along, slightly off-key, anyway. I am full of anticipation for Erin as I am belting out "Que bonitos ojos tienes" since she does indeed have beautiful eyes. I suppress an urge to follow with Aretha Franklin doing "You make me feel like a natural woman" since it was written for a different voice and gender. I sip on some ice-cold sherry, working in the kitchen in a pair of jockey shorts and a white t-shirt. The host's garments

for the event, a touch more formal, are laid out in the bedroom.

This dinner is about to be tackled with a no-holds-
barred attempt at perfection. Why, you ask? Because I
shall be in the company of Erin. The very one with the
brown eyes. I had hinted at my skills as a host and cook,
and I am now about to deliver on that threat. So, we got
flowers. We got the ice-cold Crémant d'Alsace and a
freshly made Octopus Ceviche. And we got the candles.
"Thus Spoke Zarathustra" is the second disk in the player,
intended to support the moment when the cloche is ripped
off the main course. I have done this before. Sometimes I
have been richly rewarded, and sometimes it was a total
waste. Gastronomically.

The main course will be Chile en Nogada. A complex Mexican dish with more than three ingredients, including water, and therefore not suitable for mere amateurs. Furthermore, it not the stuff gringos are served
north of the border, the enchiladas drowning in cheese
and tomato sauce, the Taco Bell garbage, the refried bean
mush. This is Real Mexican Food. As a dessert, we shall
have the flan, not too sweet, the milk steeped in rosemary.
Then flambeed in Zacapa Rum and a hint of honey. All
you horny bastards out there, lusting after Erin, eat your
heart out.

I rehearse my speech about Tonight's Specials, the
one we are all familiar with, often delivered in restaurants
by an impeccably groomed young man with a prominent,
well-defined sexual orientation. It is not always easy for
me to suppress my urge to mimic that particular style of
delivery.

We have about two hours to go. What in Louisiana
would be called pulled pork is ready in a warming dish,
all the other ingredients are chopped, measured, and lined
up in the proper sequence. *Ca s'appel mise en place.* The only
side dish is a saffron rice with some toasted, local,

handpicked pine nuts. So the label says, driven by the vendor's desire to justify the outrageous price.

The poblano chilies are roasting in the oven till the skin blisters. The pork and ten other ingredients, like dried apricots, plantains, almonds, currants—the list is long—are simmering. This then gets cooled down, and stuffed into the chili. They go back into the oven and, once hot, will be drizzled with a sauce made from ground almonds, goat cheese, and milk, topped off with pomegranate seeds. Many have responded to this dish with a standing ovation. Those that did not shall never—ever—be invited again.

The doorbell rings. Erin's on time. She floats into the entry. It's a bit chilly outside, so a cardigan hides a short, black cocktail dress. A simple, elegant necklace, a Tahiti pearl on a platinum wire, decorates her slender neck. A hopefully by now deemed undesirable ex-boyfriend went way out on that one. Is that what I am up against? No handbag. She made an effort, an exceptionally good sign. I go, "WOW." Twice. She knows she doesn't need to hear it from me, but it does not hurt.

Her first words are ". . . Man, this smells delectable. You did all that by yourself?" A man hates to have his gastronomical masculinity questioned. I plan to eliminate all future such questions, either expressed or implied. A cocky smile is all the response her comment deserves.

After a short, semi-awkward pause, we smile and hug. My guest flutters her eyelashes, pouts her lips, and twists her torso, reminiscent of movie star promo shots of the fifties. I smile, make a circular motion with my left hand, along the lines of a papal blessing, signaling for her to turn around. I share my spontaneous assessment, ". . . lovely. And the dress ain't bad either!" Both the humor and the compliment are appreciated, I can tell.

We are off to a good start.

The Crémant tastes excellent. By now the music has progressed to Billy Joel, Rod Stewart, and Tina Turner. Zorro is making a new friend; his endorsement regarding anyone who shows up at my place is valuable input. He likes Erin.

Harry Gets Suspicious

I am waiting in the bar of one of the few watering holes in Santa Fe—this is not New York City—for a drink with Erin. I am early, and she is unfashionably late. It's been two days since our dinner at my place. What I found most encouraging is the undisputable fact that she called to suggest that we did indeed need to see each other. Again. Tonight.

The U-shaped serving area on the bar is cluttered with cell phones, eyeglass cases, and a box of cigars. The chair I chose gives me a great view of the main entrance. I take notice of the cigars as an anomaly since there is No Smoking in public places in New Mexico, making me suppose that the box sits on the table because it's too large to fit in a pant pocket. It was an unremarkable dark-skinned guy in a properly pressed green shirt with the logo of a landscaping company I don't recognize that brought the cigars. It is early, long before the crowd has grown, when an even mix of middle-aged tourists and locals starts rolling in. The seats at the bar are taken mostly by guests that leave a seat or two empty, much like myself, in anticipation of the arrival either a date or hoping for some random guest to share a conversation.

I get a text message from Erin, promising that she will be here shortly, implying that she will brighten my day. Within a mere fifteen minutes the bar fills up and I face some arm wrestling to defend the empty chair next to mine. My wait is consumed by me observing the comings and goings of the patrons, a pastime that I actually enjoy a great deal.

As he saunters into the bar area, I observe the fellow who had joined the photo-shoot's crew at Maria's find a seat on the opposite side of the U-shaped bar, next to the landscaper. At first, I thought that they were there to meet and have a drink. The body language, however, suggests that they are strangers. By now, the barkeeper is getting overwhelmed with orders. Mostly for the ordinary drinks with only a few sophisticated cocktails that will take forever to create, pissing off those guests that are here for a quick drink before heading out. While I am waiting for my second Cosmo, I see that the landscaper drinks a beer, and his new neighbor gets a dry martini. I had overheard words like Vodka, olive, up and dirty, no salsa, no chips.

As time goes by, I observe the hand of the fellow I shall now and forever refer to as the Boss, toying with the wooden box of Cohibas. It is not long before the cigars disappear from view; the change of ownership has been a gradual, a subtle one. The green shirt pays up and heads out the door, leaving the acquisition of his cigars by a stranger unchallenged.

The room gets visibly brighter, at least in my imagination, as Erin closes up to me, and I receive a quick nibble on the back of my neck, sending fire through my loins.

She slides on to the seat I had defended with such success, her hand finds my knee and I hear "This a watering hole, correct?" It is indeed. "Then feed me a drink. Maybe a Campari Soda? No ice." The bartender, in a smallish bar always within earshot, says "coming up."

Erin points out that she cannot stay long; that's not what I wanted to hear but there it is. "Have to get a presentation ready. Surprise assignment. Sorry. I didn't know that when I called and lured you here." Lure away, darling, lure away.

I suppress most of my disappointment, I suppose, and I decide to assure her that all is well with "Let me assure you that your company is a delight, whether in small or in larger doses."

"Been waiting long?" No, my dear, I have not. I have been studying Humanity.

She raises an eyebrow, frowns mockingly and asks "You mean you have been checking out the women? I remember you telling me briefly what peaks your interest. I remember you emphasizing intellect as a way to sort the contenders. You realize of course that Boobs and Brains are not mutually exclusive?"

For my defense I object and say "I have not: please look around – you have no competition. Wall to wall guys. And, let me put this delicately: if all the models from the Victoria's Secret Fashion Show arrive and saunter down the runway – still no competition."

Cute smile and "So it wasn't for lack of trying, was it?" displaying well justified self-confidence. She knows that she could take home most of the attendees, male or female, if she were so inclined.

"Tell me about the Humanity you observed."

Interpreting what went down on the other side of the bar without drowning in inconsequential details requires some thought. "I ran into some clients I flew a few days ago. That group was joined by an individual I have not met before, but he sat down at their table for dinner. Tonight, he came to this bar. What got my attention tonight was an interaction with what was supposed to look like a casual rather than a planned encounter. I didn't buy it – the casual part I mean. Nobody fakes a coincidental meeting without a reason. Something smells fishy."

"Explain your definition of fishy"

I want to flirt, rather than explain my suspicions. "You said you had to leave, so let me use the precious time I have to impress you with what a *suave and debonair* a guy I am."

Erin laughs and says "I like it when you talk dirty to me" and I feel a need to point out that it was not dirty, it was French.

Some distance behind me a Mariachi band is beginning to set up. When I turn around I see a lone microphone standing in the center of a small stage. The first piece surprises me: it is dedicated to the lowly Cockroach. I turn my attention back to Erin.

We grab some finger food. We talk, we laugh. After half an hour she confesses that the time to leave has come. I see approaching lips heading my way, I turn my head – not fast enough it turns out – she misses my lips and plants the kiss on my cheek and she goes "Not quite quick enough are we tonight?"

"Trust me, I'll be ready next time."

I signal the barman; on a busy night the wait for the check can deplete a man's will to live.

An enormous woman saunters across the stage and joins the band. Half way through her rendition of El Rey, Erin looks in my direction and says "It's over." I look at her, flabbergasted, and I go "Huuh?" I have been in such a good mood and so was she. What the hell? I inquire "Please explain." She bursts into hilarious laughter and now she is ready to share the punchline and offers "The fat lady sings."

Note to Self: This one is a keeper.

Harry Alerts the Feds

I am driving up the highway to Los Alamos, past the center of town, and I take the turn across the bridge, slowing down and coming to a stop at one of the many guard booths at the Security Perimeter where identification is checked, and the purpose of the visit is questioned. I have been in and out here on numerous occasions when I had been hired to fly for any number of purposes. Inside the Lab's perimeter I have done powerline patrol, fire break inspections, and aerial photography flights to monitor construction progress; however, I was never given any kind of access badge. Flying into the restricted airspace over the Lab's vast area is complicated. They have excellent radar coverage, and they can defend themselves—I was told. They are good at safety and security: Once the engine was running and I was sitting on the ground at Los Alamos airport, I used to get a call just prior to lift off with a unique four-digit transponder code, the code that's supposed to keep the surface-to-air-missiles off my tail.

The guard is tall, lanky, and has a huge pimple on his nose that I bet is a distraction for just about anybody coming in contact with him. I hand over my driver's license and offer, "I am here to meet with a Miss Garcia in building eight. Her number is 87663."

He is not used to believing anything from anybody and looks up Miss Garcia's phone number before making the call. The call is brief and in a hushed voice that is camouflaged by the noise of the morning traffic of Lab staff arriving late for work. I am handed a poorly printed map where the guard has marked with a highlighter the turns to take, the spot to park, and the entrance to the building I am to visit. It's all amicable, no-nonsense, and professional.

I had made a call yesterday afternoon, after spending some time looking at the LANL web page to determine who to call and how to explain why I felt a need to drop by and have a talk. I ended up calling the Communications Office. I explained that I have reason to believe that I have observed behavior that may or may not represent a security concern for the Lab. I had declined to give more detail over the phone. I had written out my pitch, careful to avoid anything that would mistakenly be interpreted as a crank call from some nutcase. Considering what the Lab does and knowing a bit about the many among us who detest anything nuclear, whether they understand the topic or not, they must be getting a lot of nutcases causing problems.

After a brief hold where I was subjected to really annoying country music about the truck and the dog and the girlfriend that ran off with some biker, Miss Garcia, a lady with a most pleasant voice, came on. She responded that she would arrange for me to talk to the proper channels. Be at my office at ten sharp, I was told, the strict wording of her instructions overshadowing the charm in her voice.

It is now nine forty-eight. I find the building, park, and enter the lobby. Another guard has my name on his screen, yet he wants to see the driver's license one more time. He sits behind thick glass with a narrow slot at the bottom to pass identification back and forth. An airlock, a mechanism that allows one person at the time to enter an intermediary space that can be exited only after the door behind is closed, gets me into the actual lobby, where a well-dressed lady is waiting for me.

"I am Julie Garcia. Welcome. Find the place, alright?" She acknowledges my nod and speeds on.

"You will be meeting with two of our senior people in a few minutes, for a few minutes. One is a public relations coordinator for the security office, and the other is special agent Matt Murphy of the FBI."

As we go up a set of stairs and into a meeting room, I am greeted by Matt. He looks the part. We are just about ready to sit down when another man enters the room; he sits down without an introduction. Once all three of us are seated, Matt asks, "So, what can we do for you?"

Unable to suppress my urge to offend, I ask, "How about a cup of coffee?" knowing damn well that wasn't the kind of offer he had expressed. Federal cops don't necessarily come with a sense of humor I discover.

I start with, "There is a good likelihood that what I am about to tell you is nothing but coincidence or a misinterpretation on my part of something innocent. We haven't met before, but I am sort of known to some extent around here. I fly helicopters out of Santa Fe and have done work in the past for the Lab."

111

A raised finger from the nameless security chap, followed by "We know," saves some time. He's clearly not a big talker, but I am impressed that they made an effort to look me up.

"For starters, I'll give you the reader's digest version. I kept running into the same group of people or members thereof, and I observed behavior that may have an innocent explanation. It could also be the manifestation of something crooked being cooked up. No clear, direct link or reason to assume that it's Lab-related, but if it is, you should be concerned."

Matt suggests that I walk him through the cast of characters and the chronology. I have brought along a copy of the contract from the photoshoot and a list of names, email addresses, and cell numbers, which I pass over to him. I also toss two of my business cards on the table and begin. Always fish for more business.

"I was contracted to fly models and a camera team for a fashion photoshoot between Santa Fe airport and the Rio Grande, landing about where the tip of the Bandelier National Monument ends at the river. Quite scenic and very isolated. No road access, but there is a hiking trail that leads from the river up a steep ravine. That ravine ends on Highway 4 close to one of your gates. I believe it is marked as gate fifty-five?" The moment I say the gates number, I detect a change in the demeanor and the body language of both men.

"On any of these photoshoots, once everything is there and I shut down, I have not much to do but watch what is going on or take a nap in the backseat of the chopper. On this trip, I was confused by several indicators that made little or no sense. First: this was not a cheap operation. Flight time alone was three hours total at fifteen hundred bucks an hour. The pictures were meant for the fall mail order catalog—or so I was told, and my experience tells me that they are way late for that. This stuff is composed and then edited here, then printed in China and shipped via container for distribution in the US. Taking pictures in June will not allow mailing catalogs in September. That's number one. Number two that offended my sense of logic was the fact that one of the camera team spent most of the time scrutinizing the surrounding area, especially the trail going up the ravine."

Someone offers that the Frijoles Canyon, an old hiking trail, now washed out in a flood, fits the description.

"He also seemed interested in the rivers flow and depth, although by using a helicopter, the depth of the water is irrelevant. Maybe he is a bird watcher? A fisherman? Maybe he was as bored as I was. But then, why did he come along? The girls didn't rock my boat either. Nothing wrong with them, but their looks and moves seem amateurish. Questions?"

Not yet, I am told. Please proceed.

I proceed.

"Same day, I am having dinner with a friend at Maria's when the crew minus the girls show up for dinner as well. One new guy was now part of the group. A bit older, the leader of the pack judging by the group's body language. I recognized them, but they did not take notice of my presence."

I rub my nose, I pause, I raise my voice a tad. "Now it gets interesting. Three days later, I am sitting at a bar waiting for my date, when the New Guy or the Boss, as I like to refer to him, shows up, sitting directly opposite me between two empty bar stools. Next to some guy in a landscaper uniform. The impression I got was that they were complete strangers. Not a word was exchanged between them. The landscaper, and this made me pay attention, shows up with a wooden box with what looks like cigars. He puts that box on the table, next to his sunglasses, his cellphone, and a large bundle of keys, positioning the stuff sort of in front of the empty seat that separates the Boss and the guy with the cigars. Of course, there is no smoking in the bar.

Both have their drink—a beer and a Martini respectively. Now comes the juicy part: very gradually, the Boss takes charge of the cigars. What looks like theft is left unchallenged by the landscaper, who pays up, collects his glasses, etc. and leaves the bar. Boss finishes his drink, pays, and gets out as well. With the outline of the cigar box clearly visible in his pants pocket. It was either theft, or it was supposed to be a meeting between two people who were really just pretending not knowing each other to discreetly make the box change hands."

Both are sitting straight up, and I know I have their attention now. And now both have questions.

"Do you know where they stay?" Nope. "Any idea why they are still here?" Nope. "Did they drive a car?" Yep. "Ryder truck. The girls came in an SUV with a driver I've seen before but haven't met." The next question is, "Pee break?" Yep. They want time alone, so I take a trip down the hall. I am back within two to three minutes.

FBI speaks on behalf of the team. "First of all, thanks for bringing this to our attention. Second, congrats on your power of observation and deduction. To us, this sounds worthy of pursuit. We'd like to invite you to have lunch in our Mensa while we brief some of our colleagues with the idea of meeting again, say one PM? Right now, this early, you will have no problem finding a seat!" A piece of yellow paper changes into my hand, and I am sent to explore and possibly enjoy the gastronomical delights of a government-run canteen.

The food sucks. Worse than expected. Shepherd's Pie is the universal answer for hiding inedible ground beef in under-salted mashed potatoes. The salad is limp, and I pour way too much French dressing on it to hide the gastronomical insult the salad represents.

I am back by one. Now the group has grown to six, all male. No introduction is made. Time to show my superior sense of humor.

"So, you needed time and help to decide if I am a flake?" Matt is quick to assure me that my integrity and veracity are not in question here. I guess they must have called the fellow I negotiate contracts with when I work for the Lab. And by now, they probably have the metadata of every phone call I made from any of my phones in the last ten years. More importantly, they by now probably have the same data on every telephone whose number I passed along earlier.

Now I have a question. "Does any of this ring a bell?" No one answers, they all blush like young girls exposed to crude propositions the first time. So, you DO know something is cooking. You guys better take acting lessons if you want to fool me. "I take this as a Yes." Still no comment.

The four newcomers have some redundant questions. The meeting is wrapping up. One of the newcomers speaks up. He somehow gives off an aura of leadership far beyond Matt's. "Thank you for coming here. Let's stay in touch."

I decide that the trip home should include a detour for shopping. I stop at Home Depot to replace a stolen step ladder, some tie-wraps, a gallon windshield wiper fluid. Filling up the truck and grabbing some fresh milk plus a bag of Zorro's kibbles end the journey home.

The Feds Ask for Help

I am home late, worn out, and hungry. I mix myself a Vesper, and I munch on a few cold shrimps with cocktail sauce to tide me over till a late dinner is ready. Steak Pot Pie, a small salad—this one is crisp—and a bottle of Stella Artois. I am tempted to send a small sample of my salad to the Lab as a reference.

As I mix the drink, I punch the play button on the answering machine.

"This is Matt from the Lab calling. Please call me back at your earliest convenience. Have a nice evening." The call is announced as having come in at five-forty, and it's now eight in the evening. I decide to wait till morning since all I have is his business card with no cell number listed.

117

I turn on the TV and go to Netflix. I watch most of some episodes of *Longmire*, mainly because it is primarily being filmed here in Santa Fe, in the Valle Caldera, and Las Vegas, New Mexico. It appears that no movie or series is ever shot where it claims to play. Longmire, they want you to believe, works as a County Sheriff somewhere in Wyoming. Based on what little I've seen of Wyoming, filming the series in New Mexico seems like a good fit.

The phone rings at half-past nine. I take a deep breath so that I can yell obscenities at the caller, should it turn out to be a sales call. It is Matt, and I dispense with the vulgarities, but I let him have an overview of what I had been prepared to say. He chuckles. I am tempted to ask, "What can I do for you?" but I suppress the urge to do so. Once that question has been asked, one's option to decline the solicited favor seems to evaporate.

"We would very much like you to come back, ideally tomorrow morning. We have given our topic from two days ago some more thought and done some research. Based on our current assessment, we'd like to propose a business deal to you." He must have somehow sensed my inclination to decline and stops talking.

"Tomorrow morning will not work, I am afraid, since I am rounding up a couple truckloads of buffalo over near Cimarron and won't be back here in Santa Fe till two PM."

Matt seems flabbergasted and asks, "Who can afford to pay for a helicopter to round up livestock?" yet he quickly accepts my response pointing out that, "No cowboy, not even a smart one, meaning anyone with an IQ no less than seventy, wants to be caught riding in front of a stampeding herd of bison. Them critters are not cows, you know, they are pretty much as wild as they have been when the Indians hunted them with bow and arrow." He is one curious fellow and asks, "Who eats buffalo meat anyway?" The answer, of course, has to do with bison's meat lack of cholesterol and, for that reason, it is coveted by humans with high blood pressure and a medical history of heart disease.

He does not seem to take rejection easily. "Can you stop on the way home here in Los Alamos for an hour and a half? Not much of a detour, is it?" No, it isn't, but good business sense calls for a reluctant reply to make the Lab pay for the detour. General aviation is a high margin business but with very high fixed costs, costs like eighty thousand dollars in insurance premiums per annum, so squeezing the Feds for say an hour's worth of flying will do wonders for my weekly bottom line.

"I have been working for that ranch many times before, and they know what it costs to fly deadhead back and forth. Deadhead meaning the time it takes to reposition the aircraft to and from the ranch. So you better either pick another day or get a budget approved. Nothing less than two grand will work." I am also trying to find out precisely how motivated the Lab is to talk to me. Matt grudgingly goes, "Alright." They are motivated. No idea what the hell he wants, but for two thousand dollars, I am willing to listen all afternoon.

"So, two PM, same place?" The same place indeed.

I am intrigued and decide to leave a bit earlier in the morning, after getting across the Rocky Mountains, stopping at Raton airport to top off the tanks all the way, giving me a good three hours endurance for chasing the beasts. The new timeline calls for a wake-up call around four am, making me decide to go to bed as quickly as feasible. Flying a helicopter ten feet off the prairie floor requires an alert and rested pilot. I plan to die in the arms of a beautiful woman, most likely shot by a jealous husband, rather than in a fiery crash due to lack of attention.

I am quite sure that I haven't really slept yet when the cellphone's wake-up call yanks me from my sleep. A

119

brief, miserably cold shower, clears my head. I head out, after a yogurt and satisfactory success in forcing a reluctant Zorro into the back seat.

Harry Gets Recruited

This is going to be a different meeting than the one a few days ago. I am the first one to be led into the meeting room. Bigger, better, windowless. Two rows of seats, one row around the table, another row back against the wall. One double door, operated by a civilian holding a clipboard, checking me in. When the time comes for the rest of the attendees to show up, he will do the same with everyone, even one tough-looking guy in an Army uniform with two stars. He supposedly is from Military Intelligence, a term that's categorized as a paradox by Webster's. There is a thin folder on just about every seat.

Matt shows up ten minutes early, followed by a wingman. We shake hands, we sit down, and the wingman produces a one-page document that arrives in front of me, followed by a shiny new pen. The wingman retreats to the second row, halfway out of my sight. An almost inaudible conversation taking place behind me with the wingman seems to be dealing with refreshments that are late in arriving, just as a small tray with coffee and low and behold a Federal cookie shows up served by a magic hand.

Matt suggests that I read the document. It is short, precise, and written in government legalese; it is precisely the kind of rag that I loathe. The title informs me that this is an agreement between Uncle Sam and me compelling me to never ever talk about this, all future and the previous meeting under threat of imprisonment for every and any violation of up to and including twenty years in the Federal penal system. Visions of Waterboarding immediately cross my mind. My name and today's date are at the bottom; this thing is ready for my signature. The problem is: I am not. At least not yet.

Matt asks whether I have any questions. I do. "Pray tell, why in God's name would I want to sign this?" My reward is the smirking smile I have learned to cherish. He moves around the table and sits down in the next seat, a move that often precedes the closing argument when one is buying a car. He wants to sell me something, a job he is poorly prepared for; his daytime job is pushing paper and intimidating applicants for a security clearance, asking for favors is not his forte.

"Look, we want and need your help. All we are asking for right now is that you listen to us when we share with you much—let me rephrase that—some of what we know, what we don't know, what we plan to do about all this, and what role we'd like you to play. After we gave you what I would like to call a teaser, the minimum info we believe we can get away with, but enough for you to accept or decline to help us, you are free to finish your coffee and leave. No offense taken. Never the less, it is mandatory for us to have assurances and protection when we are revealing sources, methods, and tactics to you."

Protecting sources, methods, and tactics is SpySpeak. Next, he will tell me that my nation needs me.

"Your nation is asking for your help right now." Sometimes it is annoying to always be right.

In the days since we first met, I have casually been trying to speculate about my interpretation of what I have seen, and my best guess up to this point is inconclusive. At first, I warmed up to the notion that the people around The Boss are working for a news organization hostile to the nuclear defense program. One obvious question that nags me is why they felt it necessary to swap Cuban cigar boxes in public, yet in secret. This morning as I was flying back from Raton, my revised guess shifted to Nuke Haters gathering evidence of government incompetence and waste. Both of these bodies would have overlapping motivations. And LANL has been plagued by leaks, minor embarrassing accidents, and screwups, so collecting information centered around the most dangerous and the most expensive toys this nation owns, promises an abundant yield in exchange for a minor investment.

I hate the idea of signing that non-disclosure agreement. My curiosity and maybe a sense of intrigue and adventure would forever leave me hungry for an explanation, should I choose to take my leave now. So it would be wise to listen to their story. A prerequisite for me to acquire such intriguing insights is my signature on that one page in front of me. The words Business Proposition last night on the phone also conjured up visions of rich financial rewards and, of course, possibly a grateful handshake in the Oval Office for service beyond the call of duty. Keep dreaming, my boy.

I sign. Wingman snaps up the paper but leaves the pen. When I ask for a copy, I am told that no such copy will be forthcoming due to security concerns. All they wanted is leverage. Now they have leverage. The wingman disappears, never to surface again. Some phone calls are made. At two-twenty, a largish group starts to filter in. Whoever is manipulating this whole exercise behind the scenes had expected and was willing to accommodate a longish haggling process, now leaving me with the impression that I was a touch too quick to sign.

The fellow that had said the last word at the previous meeting sits at the end of the table, the seat where the waiter brings the check in a restaurant. Today he is in a suit. A curved, substantial nose conjures up visions of a bald eagle. No introduction is made; the price for learning who the hell is who will likely depend upon and follow a commitment of mine to play a yet undefined role in this. For the time being, I decide to think of him as the Eagle. He clears his throat, followed by warm words of welcome and of gratitude for my willingness to follow the invitation so promptly. It is now my turn to set the tone for today on behalf of all citizens called upon to help, by pushing my invoice for one hour of flight time in the direction of Matt. He doesn't even glance at it.

The Eagle opens up with, "This organization employs thousands of scientists and technicians working on both basic and applied research, mostly in physics." Designing nuclear weapons is about as applied as physics can get. "Security is a constant concern, and we spend a whole bunch of funding on security." The modesty of this statement is touching. "We have tried to map what we learned from you last Tuesday against some unexplained efforts by individuals, unknown at this time, that left us with a level of anxiety not often seen here. In short, we came upon what might be preparations for a breach of the perimeter near some of the most sensitive installations we operate. Also: in the general area in proximity to the Lab where the crime rate is very, very low, we learned that the Santa Fe Sheriff has a deputy that went missing. Might be connected? After your visit, we have made significant strides in identifying the individuals you encountered as your customers and that you observed later in a social setting. What we learned so far is of great concern. So for the moment, we are treating this as follows: we suspect what has been going on is in preparation for a raid on the Lab. We are unsure what the purpose of the raid is, and our best shots at our interpretation ranges from an attempt to embarrass us, to destroying property, right up to snatching talent, or, this is the scariest scenario, stealing nuclear components." This gets my attention: The Lab is less worried about losing a few scientists through kidnapping than losing a nuke? Once I think about it, so am I. I have a thousand questions, but this is neither the time nor the place for questions, this is the time and place to keep one's mouth shut. And to listen.

"Why are you here? We have been scouring communications; actually, that's being done out in Maryland, for a change in the level and type of chatter, one tends to observe continuously, and we found no indication that the level of chatter has changed, not since your encounter nor since us detecting intrusion preparations. For us, it is of monumental importance that we be able to get close to and understand not just what they are up to but to influence the direction their activities take. We want to set traps. We want to know who's pulling the strings, we want to understand the chain of command. We want to know who is funding this whole exercise. While they continue what they are doing, we must find a way to shut down their operation when the time is right. And we want to do this in a manner that does not alert them to the fact that we are on to them. Whoever Them is. Again, assuming that they are good at this, they will be suspicious of anyone new showing up in their environment. We—our security team—need to stay way, way back. You, however, are already in the middle of their environment. Plus, remember: they found you, you did not find them, so the level of suspicion you might encounter is low."

Now I am wide awake. Adrenalin is pouring into my bloodstream. My body feels as if I was experiencing a low sugar episode. I got it. These friendly folks here want me to become the inside man, and they want me to penetrate Them. Whoever Them is. Such undertakings sometimes end with a flag presentation ceremony in Arlington where the words 'on behalf of a grateful nation. . .' are quietly being spoken by someone in a sharply pressed uniform, shiny black boots, and with a chestful of medals.

I decide that now is an excellent time to comment without acknowledging that I got it.

"You got a playbook for this, correct? I mean: you are not designing your tactical response as you go along, right? This is not amateur hour?" I believe I have offended. That's ok. Harry is angry. If these characters turn to people like me, folks that in their world are being described as mere civilians, then things cannot be going smoothly. But maybe I better tone it down a bit. I was asked to come here with a specific purpose; they know what they are going to ask me to do. Best to make'm work for it. I am beginning to calm down. Let them explain what they would like me to do for them, very closely followed by what they plan to do for me. I distinctly remember the words . . . we'd like to propose a business deal to you . . . in last night's phone conversation.

The Eagle is not easily railed. "Look, we are mustering all the help we can get. We see you as an asset."

Thanks for the opening here. "You see me as an ass?" Groans become audible. "We see you as an asset," the Eagle repeats in a not-so-subtle tone and he therefore implicitly suggests to stay away from the comedy routine.

"A lot of wheels are in motion. This is being treated as a potential Broken Arrow Incident. If we can count on your help, then we'd like to know about it. For us, it would be beneficial to have someone close to our subjects in place. Our preference would be for you to tell us here and now if you are going to exercise your right to take a hike or if we can count on your support. I can't comment on activities we'd like you to engage in until we have a commitment from you. There have been extensive discussions among this group if we should thank you for the hot tip and from then on ignore you or if we should follow the path we are on now. Now, please tell us how you feel about what you heard so far."

"This all sounds fascinating and intriguing. I am reluctant. I have read *The Little Drummer Girl* and *Our Man in Havana*. At this point, I am unsure how I would be able to help; I do understand why you hesitate to open the Kimono further. But I must point out that I have a business to run, customers to keep and satisfy even after you guys are long gone, a dog to feed, friends to cook for." A retirement age to reach. "This might turn out to be nothing more than a minor interesting distraction, or it might turn out to be very disruptive, completely dominating my personal and commercial life or anything in between. How do I explain changes in mood, behavior, and activities to my clients, my friends, the many at the airport, and at home that know my routine?" It is dawning on me that I am dragging my heels till they smoke. Good negotiating technique. There is no way I will merely observe when I can participate. One cannot be totally risk-averse and fly for a living. "I do understand my obligation to keep my mouth shut. I do understand the concept of civic duty."

Eagle has decided. "Everybody except Harry and me, please clear the room, go take a leak or something. The guard will call you if and when you need to come back."

Al gets up, and I wish I could go to the bathroom as well. I wish someone would bring a sandwich since I haven't eaten since the yogurt at four-thirty. The Eagle taxis over to a closer seat. "All good points," he concedes. "Let's cut to the chase here. I need your help. Let me address your objections. We are aware of roughly how much your helicopter business makes. We are able and willing to hold you harmless as the legal beavers like to say." Been checking my tax returns, have we? Been listening to my phone calls, have we? "We will pay you your anticipated business income regardless if you suffer losses or not. While the case is open." Sounds great, one must hope that he has the slightest idea what those numbers might be. He pushes an envelope across.

I rip it open. I am in awe. I hear myself say, "I am in."

I am informed that under these arrangements, I deserve and will be subjected to some information about tradecraft. An assistant marches me over to another building.

As I walk into the room where the promised briefing will take place, I encounter a middle-aged lady leaving the room with the demeanor of someone taking advantage of the last chance of going to the bathroom. "Hi. I'm Jane. Be right back." I surmise that this briefing had been set up before my arrival.

There are two chairs, a small table, no paper, no pencil, no whiteboard, no telephone. The room looks like the interrogation room in a lousy whodunnit movie. I take a seat. I feel like a suspect, about to be grilled by some sweaty fat guy smoking a cigar and wearing suspenders.

Jane returns and takes the other seat. She has no accent; neither does her dress reveal whether she is a permanent local or just flew in for this briefing. She comes across as really unremarkable, bland, in many ways the homemaker who is now an empty nester, working on a second career. I was promised a briefing on what was euphemistically referred to as Spook 101, and I, therefore, expected a Pierce Brosnan clone, not the tall one from the Golden Girls.

"Sooooo— let me tell you who I am and why I am here. Please do NOT tell me who you are and why you are here. As I said, I am Jane, no last name given, and I work as a trainer for many of the intelligence and security organizations. I am freelance. I have been instructed to give a brief introduction on the topic of tradecraft. I don't know why. And I don't want to know."

I must ask: "Don't they trust you?"

This cannot be a question she gets asked a lot, I can tell. After a short pause to assemble a response, she says, "Oh, they trust me. But think about it: sooner or later I get to talk and to listen to everybody we refer to as Friends. Career intelligence officers get a lot—A Lot—of training. Friends, by comparison, get just enough so that they don't fall over their feet. If someone would disclose everything there is to be disclosed, I would then end up being one of the suspects every single time something, anything leaks out. And over time, those who end up being suspects too often end up unemployed."

My turn. Let's keep it simple: "Fire away."

"I am supposed to teach you how to exercise or how to look out for tradecraft. I don't know on which side of the fence you will be deployed, the hunted or the hunter, so I keep it a bit general. Interrupt at any time with questions, ok?" I nod.

No handouts, no PowerPoint projection, no notetaking, no audio recording. This Lady is serious about security.

After some coughing on her part, she hits the trail running. "Tradecraft is loosely defined as the art and science of being a spy, often employed to avoid detection or not leaving a trail of evidence. Examples are dead drops, if the item being exchanged is information-only, if it has no other value, such as a piece of paper with encrypted numbers on it, then a dead drop will work just fine. Dead drops are unattended, and sometimes it takes hours or days till the drop is serviced. If that piece of paper disappears, that is no big loss, and it simply gets duplicated for the second try. If the item is of value, a gun or a camera, for example, the preferred method of ownership transfer would be the exchange of identical briefcases, for example, by two guys next to each other in an elevator. Either method only works if the whole setup is not observed."

My reaction is as benign as I can muster, and that is obviously not unexpected.

"For the operative, remaining undetected is not always possible. Once detected as such or becoming a likely suspect, he will, he *should*, assume that he is being followed. When being followed, the first challenge is detecting the pursuer, and the second challenge is either to simply stop doing what one is doing or try losing the pursuer. If the path the pursued takes is predictable, the pursuer can come from behind or from the front, so it's best to make the path unpredictable. Examples, in either case, are doubling back, jumping out of a subway as the door closes, taking transportation after a long walk through an open empty space, etcetera, etcetera. But be careful: being observed taking steps that can only be explained as tradecraft is the first, unavoidable risk for any spook or crook."

How does she know that I can follow at the speed with which this is going? Will there be a test at the end?

I offer "Could you slow down a bit? Being deprived of a way to keep notes doesn't help, you know?"

"For the observer, the challenge is not to reveal that he is observing. For the observed, the challenge is to detect observation."

She pauses. "Any questions so far?" None.

The lecture continues for another two and one-half hours, at which point I am given a concise summary, just before she exits Stage Right.

Harry, Erin And Ian

I have few friends. My contact list with thousands of names does not mean much. The shortlist of animate subjects that I consider to be worthy of my affection, one way or the other, places them all over the globe. A pilot's past will tend to do that. Only a handful reside in the U.S. Southwest and just a small, select group in Santa Fe proper. Santa Fe proper, in this thinly populated state, covers anything within a one-hour driving distance—in my mind, at least. I drive because I can't afford to fly my very own helicopter, at least not for mere fun. The contact list consists of a few guys I have shared adventures with, an eclectic collection of those of the female persuasion, and a dog. The most reliable and affectionate, as expected, is the dog.

Erin and Ian have met before, but not often. Actually, only once. These two I have kept semi-apart mostly because I consider Ian's views, behavior, and appearance, as well as his well-documented success with women a threat to the very detailed and very carnal intentions I have for Erin. Pilots, in general, are a paranoid bunch; it's what keeps us alive. My well-honed paranoia also covers my sparse dating life. At this particular juncture, I do need help, however—Erin and Ian's support. I need help to somehow revitalize my short and superficial relationship with what I shall from now on collectively referred to as the Bad Boys. So, while this collides with my better judgment, I have invited Erin and Ian over to my place for a few drinks and simple dinner. No reason to spoil Ian, or more precisely, to squander my energy on his pedestrian tastes as applied to nutrition. And it is definitely not the occasion to share how I earned my reputation as a caring, charming (and persistent) host, as unleashed on Erin, with Ian.

I have no reason to assume that anyone is even remotely interested in my extracurricular activities. Other than driving out into the desert to chat, my humble home will do just fabulously for my current purposes. Ian has been instructed to shower, shave, dress, behave, and keep his greasy fingers off my soon-to-be-girlfriend. My advice furthermore covered my wish that he show up sober. Hope is eternal.

Erin arrives first. She was told, back when I called her, that Ian would take part in the tonight's festivities, and to my delight, she seemed disappointed. The unenthusiastic hug I receive under the doorframe can be interpreted in a multitude of ways, my favorite being that she wished to be alone with me. No sharing. No Ian. No Zorro.

Ian shows up next, a few minutes late, trailing the fumes of an overdose of Old Spice. I have been telling him that any woman, other than the trailer-trash he so diligently pursues, will immediately be turned off by that overpowering aftershave.

Ian must feel defensive, and says "I must interject that beer on my breath would fetch even less enthusiasm and that only Old Spice is dominant enough to provide cover for the sins involving alcoholic liquids I have already committed before my arrival."

I am pulling out my cue card that contains my recipe collection, my *aide memoire* when it comes to mixing drinks.

I open the dialog with "I can offer—you ready? — red, white, beer, gin and tonic, screwdriver." Their lack of enthusiasm prompts me to continue. "So, next on the rising scale of sophistication, you will find the Vesper, the Cosmo, the Mojito. Any takers?"

Ian's predictable response is ". . . in that sequence please." Erin turns her eyes in my direction, invisible to the not overly sensitive Ian. It is my turn to ask, "Erin, pray tell, what can I dazzle you with?" A Vesper is called for, I learn. Moral support and culinary simplicity inspire Ian to follow up with ". . . the same."

To lower my guest's expectations, I reveal that tonight's one-course meal will be Hungarian goulash and spaetzle. No second course. Inquisitive minds are told that "No, there is no dessert." Stick with the plan. Deviate if necessary.

It must be evident that there is a reason for the somewhat unusual composition of tonight's guest list. I decide to hold off till after the meal has ended. The conversation shifts between a whole bunch of topics; these range from anecdotes about past travel, about sports and we talk about mutual acquaintances. But never about politics; the range of views at our table makes touching that topic unwise.

Ian, the carnivore, has his plate cleaned long before Erin is done. He resists licking the plate. When the plates are empty, all of us switch to Cardinal Mendoza, of which fine liquid I pour sparingly, since the stuff costs a fortune.

Time for the reveal.

"I ran into a bunch of people, customers I mean, a few days ago, that triggered suspicions because of their unusual demeanor. Both of you, on separate occasions, have sort of met or learned about these characters as well." I remind Ian about the table near us at Maria's, and Erin about the two guys she just missed in the bar when we had drinks in town a few days ago. This observation being delivered without fanfare still seems to evoke some modest interest. Why is he telling us all this, they silently ask themselves?

While Ian fidgets in his seat, Erin pays attention. Ian fiddles with the cutlery. I continue to summarize what had transpired in the last few days: the flight, my visit to the Lab, their solicitation for help.

Erin interjects with "What kind of help?"

"Hang around nearby, be a resource" I disclose. I skip the details of who is under suspicion of what potential and scary misdeed that may be in the planning stage; my constraint being driven by the memory of the piece of paper I signed, the document that is my direct path to a substantial prison term if I am caught leaking information that has been deemed classified. By now, it must be dawning on my guests that this invitation, the meal, and the disclosure must have a purpose other than to provide for a full stomach and an alcohol fogged brain.

"I have been asked to find ways to continue the relationship with that group. The term used was Snuggle Up. Now my view is that any upcoming snuggling will not involve these characters." Erin gets the implied flirt and only partially suppresses an emerging blush. Why does a woman like her still blush like a virgin?

134

"If I show up solo, hat in hand, to offer continued aviation services etcetera, such offers might be considered a sign that their activities have been compromised. And that would neither be productive, nor in my best interest. If I show up in the company of a desirable woman" —she heard me— "or some scruffy, disreputable character like Ian, here" —he scoffs at that description— "a more innocent explanation should come to their mind first." Even Zorro thinks that was funny. "Hence, I am soliciting your excellent company, on a few select occasions, to help me camouflage my dishonorable intentions."

Trying to keep the tone light and non-threatening might help gloss over the obvious omissions in my story. Ian is right on top of this: "You mean you intend to use us as decoys? Or even more despicable, and I am shocked at your lack of compassion, as bait?" The smirk on his face is proof that he is not really serious. Ian is trying to stir trouble, a skill that he considers having a splendid command of. I am beginning to regret having invited him since, if he were not here, Zorro might be on the living room sofa by now. Considering that I have conflicting objectives for tonight, I would accept that outcome as well. Erin has neither questions nor comments. Both know me well enough to anticipate a reason for the tease, they haven't heard it yet.

This is not going all that well. Trying to calm Ian, and as a preemptive measure put Erin at ease, I reply, "You watch way too much television. I am being asked by some law enforcement investigator, who thinks I can help, since A: I went to them with information, and B: because I am already on the radar of those who have caused suspicion. The expectation is that this will all turn out to be a waste of federal funding on a minor scale. My primary interest is growing my relationship with the Lab. They sometimes use my services, they pay on time, and best of all, they don't haggle. Being helpful here might grow my business. So, I can afford to feed more elaborate meals to my guests."

I am not going to tell them about the game camera at Gate 55 or about how big this investigation has become. I won't tell anyone that the Feds are scared shitless about what is known or exposed, and even more fearful about what is not yet known. I am not about to emphasize that approaching the Bad Boys while cooperating with the Lab puts me right in the middle of two opposing parties, both of whom will see me as a disposable participant in a high-risk chess game.

If things go sour for me: no widow to ask questions, no one writing letters to a senator. Only Zorro to howl at my grave. Let's keep a lid on it. At this point, the Lab knows merely that a group of individuals wasted some money on a photo shoot, and the Lab knows that someone mounted a camera right across the street from the only gate where fissionable nuclear material comes in and goes out—no proven connection between the two. Only the suspects would know what they are up to. Unless of course, those assigned to keep me in the loop are busy keeping me out of the loop. I have no illusion that access to an unlimited number-crunching power in Maryland has been put to good use, and I am confident that a picture of what is going on here must gradually emerge. My valued client, the crooks, must have paid for hotel rooms, meals, flights in and out, car rentals, made phone calls, sent and received emails, and browsed the Net and therefore left a trail that must resemble a four-lane highway. It is reasonable to assume that the Bad Boys have no idea that they are being watched, watched from a safe distance. Mostly— I am the closest watcher. The fact that most often it's the tail that gets hit, not the lead, is something one learns in basic training. That's the good news since I am the lead.

Time to ask the question, "Can I count on your support? All I expect is that if we are out and about, and I do something unexpected that you do not ask stupid questions."

Erin moves as if to help with meal clean-up. I discourage that. Sharing the kitchen drives me batty, Erin or no Erin. Ian flicks his napkin at my dog as if to start a tug of war game; tonight, for some reason Zorro is not so inclined.

And Then There is the Huey

The Bell Huey was a helicopter built during the Vietnam war; it was used extensively as a transport, a gunship, and as an ambulance during that war. Non-commissioned officers whose previous experience ranged from driving a tractor to riding a surfboard received a couple hundred hours of flight training before being sent to Southeast Asia. If that seems inadequate, we must remember two facts: the Huey is straightforward to fly, AND Huey pilots had a limited life expectancy in Vietnam, requiring a steady stream of replacements. Mass producing green pilots demanded efficiency and an eye on cost and thus on flight time.

I got into Hueys long after we lost that war and long before we managed to start the next one. I enjoy

139

flying them; I am even willing to forgive the lousy airspeed in exchange for a load carrying capacity that is daunting. Huey's are the DC3's of rotary wings: They will never go away, it seems.

The white and blue bird sitting on the ramp at Santa Fe airport was a newer, more powerful civilian version of the Huey. The airworthiness certificate and registration would show that it was a Bell 205A++ if the documents were visible from the outside of the locked aircraft. It was certified as less than eleven thousand pounds max takeoff weight, although it is capable of carrying a lot more than that. The reason for the voluntary limitation has to do with the FAA imposed requirement that anything above that weight requires a type certificate for that particular model, along with frequent training and check rides for the pilot to prove that he is proficient in operating it. Operators that have a whole bunch of pilots flying a whole bunch of different aircraft are not enamored by the cost of recurrent training and check rides eating away at their slim profit margin. In essence, commercial helicopter operations are a highly competitive business. The exact logic why proficiency is less of an issue at the lower weight shall always remain a mystery to most of us who do not work for the federal government. The only real difference between lower or high gross weight is the size of the crater the aircraft makes when things go wrong. A stenciled decal on the side of the bird reveals that it is owned by some outfit in Oklahoma in the business of leasing aircraft to operators who do not have the capital nor the available credit to own one themselves. I peek through the window in the sliding door and spot a fire-spitter and an assortment of cables to be attached to a Bambi bucket for water drops. The bucket itself is probably in the cargo hold somewhere in the dark back of the cabin. A peek through the left window shows a nice, clean, uncluttered flight deck, devoid of the usual pile of charts, checklists, time-tracking forms that are the hallmark of a helicopter that works for a living. The usual explanation for such a display of good taste is often less a question of crew discipline than of a bird delivered by a ferry crew hired by a client that expects excellent and speedy service.

The Huey must have arrived overnight. I've lusted after having a Huey, but not the fuel bill it will generate, for a long time. I turn my attention to today. I walk over to the Long Ranger.

Today's job for the Long Ranger consists of flying along a power line between Albuquerque and Farmington, a straight-line distance of about a hundred and fifty nautical miles. At a cruise speed of 30 knots, a speed at which the observer in the second front seat can easy check for existing or impeding damage to the mast, the insulators, the cables or identify bird's nests, would take about five hours.

The problem with that plan is the endurance of this aircraft is about three hours, with no fuel available along the way. There are three solutions to this predicament: fly faster, bring a fuel truck to the halfway point—somewhere in the middle of nowhere, or stop the inspection and make a run for fuel at a much higher speed, either back to Albuquerque or ahead to Farmington before returning to pick up where the inspection was interrupted. Blasting by the power line towers at a high speed makes it difficult to spot problems, so that is out. From the power company's perspective, hauling fuel by truck out to the desert is the most economical option. Let us remember however, that this decision is up to the pilot/operator, and his economic interest —I am selling flight time, not distance covered—is at odds with the best interests of the power company. One should also not forget that the observer will be munching a sandwich while in the air, a privilege not within reach of the pilot.

Dashing ahead to Farmington is the preferred response, since the nearest restaurant while the fuel is being pumped is very close by. Among non-aviators the question most often interjected at this point in the story is why anyone would want to pay the kind of money it costs to fly when the terrain itself poses not many obstacles for a ground vehicle to perform the same mission. Two answers quickly reveal why a ground vehicle is not a pleasant or productive option. A: it is harder to see the top of the tower from the ground than from five feet away with the rotors turning a mere five feet above the top wire, and B: and this is the killer—a helicopter does not have to stop every half mile to fumble for keys and unlock a ranch gate, drive through and lock the gate again once the car has driven past the fence. Using a ground vehicle requires a staff of two, the driver and the poor bastard who gets to climb in and out of the truck all day long. And the average speed now drops to less than five miles per hour, making the inspection of the full run of the transmission line go on for about 40 hours—in theory. This particular power transmission line goes through virtually uninhabited desert-like terrain with no food or shelter anywhere. This implies that at about one or two in the afternoon the truck must start heading either back or forward to the nearest settlement with fuel services, making the trip just about twice as long. Consequently, doing the patrol by ground vehicle takes two guys and a truck two weeks for what the helicopter does in one day. Still think it's a luxury?

I am a good hour into the flight from Double Eagle airport, where I picked up the guy from the power company, that in so many ways allows me to eat prime steak, when my pager buzzes. I don't recognize the phone number of whoever I am expected to call. I still use a pager because they work better in the boonies than cell phones. Ten minutes later, my spotter Jonathan wants me to land so he can get out and look at a pole that has been sitting in a puddle for some time. He wants to list that pole for replacement before it comes down in a storm. I use the time with the engine power all the way down to idle to prepare and submit a text message promising a call by afternoon. Pressing send gives me hope that at some spot along the way, there will be some cell service. I am assured that at the latest during lunch in Farmington, the message will go out.

Today I brought along a sandwich since I know from previous flights that Jonathan does not eat lunch, and he grows impatient when I choose to take Signature Flight Support's courtesy van to the nearest Subway. Once the spotter and I had developed a relationship, once we have learned about each other's pet peeves, I find it best not to rock the boat. I am in the service business, after all.

It is almost five in the afternoon when I am back in Santa Fe, and while a kind soul tows the bird back into the hangar, I let Zorro out for a pee and then quickly sit down in front of my calendar.

The number from the pager rings twice, and a self-assured male picks up with "Harry, how's your day going. It's John from the photoshoot. Thanks for the quick response. Question: do you fly Hueys?"

Do I fly Hueys he asks? Of course, I fly Hueys, but I am even more eager to fly the Long Ranger. Flying someone else's bird while one's own Long Ranger is sitting in the hangar does not satisfy my more carnivorous business instincts. "I do, but my Ranger costs half as much per hour. What's up?"

He continues, "You probably noticed the Bell 205 sitting at the ramp. Before it goes to a firebase, we want to use it locally. For that, it's cheaper to pay you, say a hundred bucks an hour, rather than fly in our chap from the East Coast."

Well, I see his point. "What's the job, and when does it go down?"

I get an unsatisfactory "Don't know yet. We will be able to give notice, about forty-eight hours or so. But once

143

the show is on the road, we won't have any flexibility regarding the timing."

This is a good time for quick thinking. There isn't much on the schedule for the next few days; actually, it's downright barren for a while.

"Wellllll, if you want me to be standby, we can do that, but I will be billing you a minimum of four hours a day. There are always walk-ins, and I would have to send them away." My prediction is that this will make the deal go away. Negative! He wants an agreement for signature! I should have asked for five hours minimum. Too late now.

"When's the paper ready, and where can we pick it up?" he replies.

In the age of email, who the hell picks up actual paper? "You want it emailed instead?" Nope, he wants my home address for a pickup by courier. Not so quick my boy.

"I have an office at the airport. The motorhome? Outside of the hangar? The envelope will be there by eight AM tomorrow. Check with the desk at Signature if I am out." Home address, my ass.

Harry Reports Back To LANL

I am heading back home, driving the long way around to pick up flowers, cereal, milk, and re-plenishments for the bar. If there ever is such a thing as rush hour in Santa Fe, I am spared that particular agony tonight. It's a rare day when one tends to get stuck between light changes anywhere north of Albuquerque. Having flown traffic helicopters over the Los Angeles ba-sin has left me with a permanent distaste for following cars with brake lights coming on every few seconds. From five hundred feet above one of the endless LA freeways, the most cost-effective method for guessing traffic speed, not easy if one is doing one hundred knots groundspeed, is observing the ratio between brakes on and brakes off. And at five in the evening, the 405 looks like a parking lot. Not so in this area.

It takes me all of forty-five minutes, traffic being light, the road surface dry, and most of the traffic lights in my favor. Seasonal temperatures prevail, and everything is bone dry since it has not rained or snowed in any significant amount in four months.

I suppose that light to moderate paranoia is called for since I am stuck in the middle of a thriller between two interested parties with opposing objectives, neither of them trustworthy. Halfway through the shopping trip, it dawns on me that I am presented with a unique opportunity to try wild lane changes and U-turns in order to establish whether I'm being followed or not.

I try to remember Jane's lecture on measures designed to make a shadow reveal itself. Blinking left and turning right may expose someone tailing you, but that maneuver will leave little doubt as to the motive behind the movement, so that's out. As I drive past supermarket parking lots, gas stations, and dry cleaners, I patiently wait until the traffic behind me is light, and the nearest car is five hundred feet or so back. It is a black Camaro with the paint having gone matt and grey in the sun. The owner inadvertently managed to make the car easy to spot by having whitewall tires on the back and black tires on the front axle, and as an added convenience, the driving lights are not the same brightness left and right.

I enter a parking lot of a strip mall, and the Camaro whizzes by without slowing. The next vehicle behind him is turning into the same mall. It must be time to continue with the evasion. As I drive erratically through the parking lot, rejecting available spots because they are too narrow, too shallow, or too far away from the dry cleaner, I see the car find a place in front of a hair salon, and a young woman with a toddler climbs out and disappears inside. Through the window, I see her hugging one of the workers, thus pretty much ruling her out as a suspect. Just to be sure, I move into a spot some distance away and wait. She is getting her hair done. It takes mere minutes, and she is reclining her head back over a sink on the receiving end of hair wash and with it has lost the option of coming out after me. Conclusion: I am not being followed.

The phone rings. The caller ID reveals that it's Eagle.

"Heard from them?" No "Hi, how are you," no "You know who this is."

"I have heard." He is not surprised. They are listening to my calls!

He asks, "Will you be home in ten minutes?" I definitely will be home by then. "I'll see you there." And he is gone.

This briefest of interactions reveals some disturbing insights. Namely, not only have they—the Feds —tapped my phone, but I have reason to assume that they also follow the movements of my cellphone, based on Ping data. Otherwise, he would have asked about my whereabouts. Yet when dialing that prompt phone call, he already knew where I was and where I was heading.

As I pull into my spot in the driveway, a white, somewhat dented, windowless minivan, promising twenty-four-hour emergency plumbing services in two languages is already sitting there. No antennas. No hubcaps. Eagle gets out, and Al comes out the other side. Eagle is dressed for the job: jeans with rusty spots, some tears, and riding low enough for his butt crack to show in the best of plumbers' tradition.

Al is carrying a tool chest. I greet them with the friendly smile of a man uncertain why luck was bestowed upon him, and a construction service operator found it in his heart to actually show up. I open the door and wave them in.

I feel a need to express my lack of enthusiasm about what I deduced. So, when a couple of beers are requested, I ignore the request. My general rule is to withhold refreshments when these are sought rather than being offered.

"You are listening to my calls, and you are tracking my movements," I hiss. "Are you by any chance also having me followed?"

Al quickly puts that notion to bed. "Way too risky. If the other side follows you as well, our surveillance efforts might become exposed. If they get caught following you around, that's not a big problem, but if our guys behave flatfooted, that would be less desirable."

Eagle confirms some of my analyses by stating, "So they want to hire you to fly the Huey." This is sobering. I am being recorded.

"Actually, they want me on stand-by to fly the Huey now that it's here and before it goes to a firebase. That would explain the Bambi bucket and the ping-pong dispenser." I feel a need to explain how one starts a fire from a helicopter.

"I suspect that this will turn into a bait-and-switch. They are building a relationship. Perhaps make me break some minor laws to see if I can be corrupted. Then blackmail me into doing whatever job they have in mind and that I am being groomed for." And once I have become redundant and a liability, pay me off with a single .22 caliber shot into the back of the head?

Eagle and Al briefly ponder the merits of my thoughts. Al wants to know if I am aware of a simple, reliable way of stopping the Huey from flying. In such a way that I am not the obvious culprit. I am aware of such a method: loosen the nut over the line that sends ambient air pressure to the fuel control just a little bit, since that had happened to me years ago; the result is that the engine will not come up to full power and the bird will promptly be grounded.

Eagle proposes, while gently massaging his chin for higher quality logic, that "The Huey scares me. We have no idea what they are up to, but the Huey gives them a lot of mobility and options such as flying in and out of monitored airspace, up and down ravines under the altitude for our radar to see it. So, let's decide here and now that as the threat becomes clearer or when they ask you to do something crazy, you will use that trick to ground it. Ground vehicles are slow, have to follow roads, and are easily blocked by a road closure."

Sounds like a plan to me. I must ask myself: do I sign that deal we negotiated? The fact that is unnecessarily generous fits the overall picture. I do like the income however.

Al impatiently interrupts with, "Will you stop worrying about getting paid? Please? We told you we would come through for you?"

"Do we sign or not? Can I get a straight answer for once?"

Eagle is not used to having his judgment questioned and makes that clear by barking," You will sign."

Yessss Sirrrr.

Erin Spends the Night

Six AM is not my best hour. Never has been. I'm up this morning at this ungodly hour, full of energy and cheer because tonight I'll have another shot at Erin's libido. She'd left me a message while I was out flying, asking for a callback in a voice that, at least in my fertile imagination, held a promise of deviant pleasures.

The grocery shops that are open for business at six in the morning might not do justice to my cuisine; I was, however, shopping for me, not for my guest. That will come later, once I devise an approach.

I ran into Erin yesterday in the frozen dessert section of the supermarket before I could make the return call. I don't appreciate getting caught shopping for ready-to-eat desserts, after bragging about homemade

151

Everything. Her face lit up, while my contribution was a surprised face followed by what she later described as a leering grin.

I got a hug. It is incredible how much one can learn from a simple hug. There is the Minimum-Body-Contact hug that signals nothing more than mutual recognition. To be used when not remembering the name nor the occasion. Not really an ounce of affection there. The Near-Max-Body-Contact hug is yet quite another thing altogether. That is the kind of hug that could result in a romantic interlude. Erin's hug was somewhere about midway between but made up for it by letting her lips brush mine. The duration of the hug is another measure of affection or intent. She held my embrace for not quite eight seconds, just like at the rodeo. I was delighted.

Today, while under the shower, I contemplate the proper allocation of time and resources to the various phases that make up such an endeavor. This project consists of an open-ended evening to provide a chance to bask in one's glory.

I am a planner. Clearly, this second dinner date calls for a different resource allocation than the first. Drinks should be relaxing. Actually, it should lessen or remove any undue inhibitions. Long Island Ice Tea comes to mind. On second thought, that's overkill. I reprogram myself for a Mojito. The music better be sensual, a single piano with a sax playing bar music perhaps. Or Clayderman. No, not Clayderman: his music gives me a spontaneous toothache because my dentist plays that artist over and over again. I decide to risk being suggestive in my choice of music: Anyone who's seen the movie 10 with Bo Derek is expected to remember what Ravel's *Bolero* is supposed to initiate.

Ideally, the meal should be something easy to eat without cutting or chopping: a stew, a soup. My bouillabaisse will fit the bill: Not much time wasted in cooking or in spooning it up. A baguette with rouille—a little garlic can add spice to match the evening.

She is expected for dinner at seven. So, I must remember to light the candles in the bedroom just before seven. Just in case my plan works. Some kind soul had bestowed upon me the care of some ancient candles that were marketed as creating the illusion of an afternoon at the beach. Just what New Mexico calls for, located about a thousand miles from the nearest shore. To make sure I don't run out of time, new sheets and a thin, rolled-up comforter with the mandatory four pillows piled up against the headrest wink back at me. The bedroom was in great shape even before I stepped into the shower.

By noon I am done writing and emailing proposals from calls and emailed-in prospects, many of whom will never be heard from again. Those who haven't used aircraft for their business or pleasure often fail to understand how it is possible to charge forty cents a second for flight time. In the out tray are some checks to those who have not yet discovered online payments. The two lanky, pimple-faced teenagers that I trust with the Long Ranger for cleaning inside and out, do not have a bank account. I like their work, but safety comes first. I always disconnect the battery before letting them touch it. Accidentally running up the engine inside the hangar would spoil my relationship with the other tenants.

After a chili dog, I found my way to Whole Foods. The only place in town for seafood. The Northern Rio Grande is not known for its fish. Black mussels in the shell, peeled shrimp, some scallops and a beautiful piece of sea bass that will be cut into smallish pieces are procured. At home, I prepare the rouille and the bouillon. The fire-roasted bell peppers come out of the fridge and join the cherry tomatoes in a bowl. *Mis en place*—ask Bourdain.

My thoughts, as I sit for a few minutes to go over the preparations, center around the insight that I know very little about Erin. She had not volunteered much be-yond "Never married, no children, moved around a lot, recently moved to Santa Fe." I had asked when we first met at the meeting in Albuquerque "And so, where did you move from?" and I got a non-committal "Overseas." When I asked where she lived, she gave me an address in the Loft Development, a slightly aging complex of condo apartments. When I hinted, much later, that maybe one day I would love to see the place, her answer was surpris-ingly politically incorrect: "When I am at someone's place, and I feel a need to leave, that option is always open. When the guest is over at my place, that option is sort of no longer available." I decided not to pursue that line of ques-tioning until I have a better sense of why she is so oddly reluctant to open up. All this caution slash paranoia could well be the result of some relevant unpleasant experiences with admirers more skilled than I, that preceded me.

Zorro senses her approach first, without ever di-vulging if it's sound, smell, or sight he uses to categorize the arrival of my infrequent visitors. She's a few minutes early, so I yell through the closed door, "It's open." I duck into the bedroom to change into a pair of beige linen slacks and a matching short sleeve shirt. The tropical look. No shoes. I am also wearing an apron until dinner is actually served. No greasy spots on my pants tonight—this also of-fers also protection from a possibly embarrassing erection. Just in time, I remember to light the scented candles.

Emerging into the kitchen, I stop in awe: she is sit-ting on a bar-stool, legs crossed, high heel shoes, wearing a short cocktail dress. This one is red. I am surprised: why would any woman have two or more cocktail dresses that look similar but are a different color? She smiles that won-derful radiant smile of hers, slides off the stool, and floats across the room into my arms. As my left hand travels down her back, I discover that I will be the beneficiary of cleavage both in front and in the back, since the dress seems to have no back at all. I hold up her arm with one hand soliciting a spin type dance move, and once she complies, I take in the complete package. When I ask "And why are you wearing your dress backwards?" she just smiles.

"Hi." Pause. She tilts her head a little, waiting for a somewhat more meaningful conversation. *I am dumbstruck.* "I am dumbstruck." She had gone all out, including the jewelry, the lashes, and faintly smoky eye makeup. I am keenly aware that I do not deserve any of this but decide to suppress any such admission.

Erin is about to step forward as I hold up my hand, signaling her to stay put. "I need to admire all this in that favorable light for just a moment longer."

"Take all the time you need," she says with a mischievous smile. And so I do. There is a point, however, when admiring looks transition into a stare, so I settle into one corner of the sofa, giving her lots of options on where to sit. She tucks one leg up on the couch, sitting on it right about on the perfect spot, close enough for me to take in the perfume she is wearing. It is my considered opinion that everything else she's wearing is redundant. Her hand rests on my shoulder, and I conjure up the faint illusion of harp music when I hear her say, "I missed you." Zorro's head comes up once he senses the near-instant raise of my body temperature.

I am way too old to explain the knot in my throat that I need to dislodge before I manage to respond with "I had no idea how much I missed you till you just walked in the door" in a hoarse voice.

She's quick: "And I thought our budding relationship was based solely on mutual overlapping intellectual interests."

The time to correct such an erroneous assumption with "Hell no. It's mostly driven by raw, insatiable lust." I look at her. She heard me. See: it might be possible to project undesirable or unacceptable intent in these words—yet she is still here.

She leans back into the crook of my arms and mumbles something about how an adult beverage would come in handy right now. No kidding. I hesitate and then explain that it is not feasible to assemble a cocktail from my current position on the sofa without losing any of the advantages I enjoy with her in my arms. She sits up straight, pulls a fake stern face, and wordlessly points with an outstretched arm to the bar in the kitchen. I am up and pouring at the same time that I suggest that "I have no idea what the world record for an amateur barman's time is to assemble a Mojito. But I ache to beat it."

I hear her over the music, asking, "When are we going flying again?" I somehow fail to respond in time, so the question is posed a second time. The time to be delicate, yet firm has come. "There will be some ferry flights coming up in the next two weeks. These tend to offer stick-time opportunities, all paid for. Other than that, it is pretty slow right now. And I really can't afford *pro bono* outings." She takes rejection well, despite a lack of much experience in being rejected she assures me.

The moment the drinks are ready, and as I carry in the tray she gets up, stands behind me and grabs her glass from beneath my arm at the very moment I turn in the other direction. The resulting collision creates a fountain of rum, sugar, sparkling water, and mint that splatters all over both our fronts. We both say, "Shit. Sorry" at the same time, and she chuckles at my part of the mutual display of clumsiness.

I look down at my shirt and then at her dress. We are essentially dripping wet. She does the same herself. It's pretty evident that the garments will have to come off. A gleam in her eyes—and do I detect a blush? —tells me that our thoughts are being synchronized. Erin takes my glass and pours what's left of my drink into her glass, and she takes my hand in her free hand and points towards the back of the house, saying, "I believe that the shower is that way."

I reach past her and open the door to the hall that leads to the shower and, and better yet, the bedroom. She takes note of the pillows, the candles and inhales the wonderful scent they emit, turns a bit, looks at me with an amused expression, and says, "Was this no accident?" *It was; it actually was.*

"If it was not an accident, then all you had to do was ask."

The Decoy

This particular briefer is essentially a Robert Oppenheimer look-alike, minus the pork pie hat. The room is filled with the more or less complete command structure of the Broken Arrow Response Team. We are here to learn how far the group has come in defining a response to the mess we are involved in.

I must be here because it supposedly is my job to keep a close look at the "opposition," and I am expected to map whatever I can learn about what now generally is referred to as The Crooks against the plans of this team. Why? Once the breach is initiated we want The Crooks to proceed with their plans, so we can catch not just the foot soldiers but the leadership as well. A dummy Pit is going to be placed "within reach" inside the gate area, momentarily unguarded. A trap. A decoy. Knowing when the time has come to set that trap represents the major challenge. For non-scientists, a dummy with some intentionally applied weak gamma emitter cannot be distinguished from the real thing.

I see a lot of problems with this plan. While I am beginning to see the strategy at work here, this approach will require that a fair number of activities undertaken by the other side in this conflict will misfire. At the same time, from a defensive viewpoint, just about every step taken must succeed. An occasional glance by Eagle in my direction, soliciting comment, is met with cagey silence. This is not my world. In my world anticipation, planning, keeping options open as long as possible are rewarded with success. In their world, excessive force, massive overkill, are sometime used to make up for lack of a good plan. I refuse to take on any bets on the outcome in our situation.

Not everyone's personality in this meeting is cut from the same cloth. I stick out like a sore thumb: no military background. Harry Reasoner is given credit for "This is why being a helicopter pilot is so different from being an airplane pilot, and why in generality, airplane pilots are open, clear-eyed, buoyant extroverts, and helicopter pilots are brooding introspective anticipators of trouble. They know if something bad has not happened it is about to." Harry Reasoner ends a sentence with a preposition? I am shocked.

The briefer picks up the pace a bit. He should have skipped to the chase by now; most attendees know what's coming.

"LANL manufactures exact replicas of a PU239 Pit. Inert dummies. Why do you ask? Both for machine calibration, quality control, and for CNC operator training, these grapefruit-size hollow spheres allow for situations that would never be allowed to occur with a live Pit. I mean, dummies get passed around among students in training classes. Dummy pits are manufactured from

U238—depleted Uranium. It is cheap, abundantly available. Tons of this stuff comes out of the Oak Ridge Tennessee Uranium enrichment facility. Enrichment separates the isotopes; specifically, it removes a tiny amount of the Good Stuff, U235 from the, from a fission viewpoint inert, U238. Depleted Uranium is used to make armor-piercing munitions for the military. Because of its huge atomic weight, the kinetic energy in a bullet from that stuff does unbelievable damage. This ammunition is delivered by such aircraft, known as the A-10 tank killer. A nasty combination, ask any Iraqi tank commander."

A fraction of those represent the age group of Iraq war veterans. I see a nod from one, as he recollects his experiences in the desert.

"So, what's the difference between an actual "live" Pit that will go into a weapon and an inert dummy? They look the same, weigh almost the same; the most significant difference is going to be markings to the effect that this is a dummy. The Pit is surprisingly massive for its size. It's stored and transported, one per a plastic case, with a combination lock, the inside of which is lined with a thin layer of a cadmium alloy to capture neutrons that escape spontaneously from the decaying U235. Even when dozens of these boxes are stacked and stored together, criticality cannot occur."

Someone carries a dull grey box that looks much like what in the seventies was called a beauty case, just as promised, into the room. Once a shiny, grapefruit-size sphere coated in a dull hue of gold emerges from the box, it is passed around among the meeting participants. This one is clearly marked as an inert dummy. Somewhere in the back of the building, in a safe, sits one just like this, but decorated with the markings you would expect from a real weapon, ready to be placed in the back of a small SUV in plain, dull, grey-green paint. The whole idea is to keep that vehicle ready until an attempted breach is detected. Rolling it out and then having the staff disappear inside should give an attacker a shot at stealing the stuff with no need for violence against humans.

The GPS satellite-linked tracking device is not much bigger in diameter than a silver dollar and no thicker than an eighth of an inch. Someone from the mechanical shop has peeled back the cadmium lining enough so we can see the hole where the tracker will be hidden, a hole just big enough to hold the tracker.

We learn that "another hollow space, slightly larger, also on the inside of the box, hidden by the liner, will hold the battery."

I decide to earn my keep by asking pertinent questions: "How long does the battery last?"

The reply "three days or so" is, of course, eliciting groans of frustration.

"Who will track it?" I ask. Silence.

"Someone should be, will be, must be tracking it?" Silence. I am getting into a sour mood. "If we lose sight of the vehicle with the box, and we will at some point, it might just be me that loses sight of it and I need to know who I can call."

I am told that "Never mind if you lose sight of it: It's a dummy, you dummy." I am fittingly offended.

Now our attention is directed to the need for air cover. Drones are a spook's best friend, I am told. Unless the spook is female, then that slot is occupied by diamonds. A seemingly endless discussion develops, contrasting the advantages of using cheap, hard to spot drones with very limited endurance versus using helicopters, expensive, noisy, easy to spot but with good endurance.

I feel inclined, even emboldened to put in my five cents: "I must declare that I view drones with great disdain. Why? You have to guess ahead of time where they will be needed. They must not take off until the very last moment since the maximum flight time will be fifteen minutes or so. They are not useful for the pursuit of a fast-moving object. They need a signal from the ground using line-of-sight, so they are of no use for following vehicles on a road or chasing targets on foot down ravines. Helicopters can follow a target visually, can keep chasing it till the fuel runs low."

We haggle over the option of leaving a helicopter parked at the LANL helipad. Or are we leaving it at the Santa Fe staging area instead? We keep going in circles, since the suspects are known, but not their plan, not the timing, not the objective. This predicament applies to all efforts such as deployed human resources, ground vehicles, prepared roadblocks. Finally, a decision is reached.

We are told that since we don't know if, when, and where this might go down, we will leave some of the local manpower and ground vehicles specific to the fighting of the current crisis hidden out of sight inside the LANL perimeter. "We can do this open-ended," they say. I interject that nothing is sustainable open-ended. I am being informed that Uncle Sam can—we've been dicking around Afghanistan for more than a decade now.

All air assets will continue to be hidden in the hangar at Santa Fe airport. We take a breather, many of us looking around the room for the water cooler.

Eagle thanks me for my mild contribution. He walks me to the water cooler, turns and says "About the drones: I realize that you have a dog in this fight, but you might be right. Let me think about it." Conclusion: Eagle believes me; he also suspects greed as the motive for my advice.

"Now that we have gone over the preparation, let us talk about what we will trigger once an attempted attack or breach has been detected."

Word must have gotten out that something significant is cooking because the number of new faces that show up for these meetings, all by invitation, keeps growing.

A tall fellow, in civilian dress, sitting in the back row along the wall gets up and pins a large map on the corkboard. He looks like a cop but offers no insight as to who he is and why he was chosen to lecture us on geography. Since not everyone in the room can be expected to know the roads in the area, we get a well prepared ten-minute-long lecture describing the road system within a thirty-mile radius or so.

Al gets up and joins the speaker in front. The two sort out the next part via eye contact, and after a brief pause, the Cop offers, "Let me take it from here." Al sits down again. "We will need some time to figure out what the hell is going on, and that requires that we contain whatever threat we are facing. Lucky for us there are very few ways to get in and out of the greater Los Alamos area. We believe that the forest service roads can initially be ignored since all of the ones inside the inner ring are dead ends. And in lousy condition."

The senior of the two from the Forest Service is initially offended, yet after a few seconds he concurs with a nod. The Cop continues, "Let us use the playbook for prison breaks; let us be prepared to set up two concentric circles of roadblocks. We have demonstrated during training that we can do that real quick. Looking outbound at the various roads," he pauses, and then says, "Let's block County Road 502 right after the merger with highway 4. On the other side, let us block highway 4 just before the Cuba turn off." All eyes follow the laser pointer. We learn about elevation change, anticipated driving speed, existence, or lack of guard rails. He glances around and taps

164

the map. "Now let us look at the outer ring. Why set up an outer ring? If we are too slow to get there in time and the culprits are outbound past the point we have chosen for . the inner circle, a second set of roadblocks about one hour drive away from the Lab will give us a second shot. And this may come as a surprise to whoever is behind this."

A brief discussion establishes that a significant number of road closures will be needed since anyone that made it past the inner ring now has a whole bunch of choices as to which road and direction to take.

The cop elaborates. "It starts with County Road 30 towards Española, and the further away one gets from Los Alamos, the nastier the planning gets. Blocking major interstates like I25 going north to Denver and south to Albuquerque or even worse, I40 going east towards Amarillo or west towards Flagstaff, is likely to get reported on the radio and any traffic jams we would create could well show up on GPS devices with traffic reporting. There is no point in advertising on how far one can get on any given escape route."

A voice in the dark back of the room pipes up, "I have an idea: going south on I25 towards Albuquerque just before La Bajada is a never used Inspection Station for commercial traffic. Good place. No residential or commercial buildings anywhere near. In the other direction, a similar situation is available near Glorieta pass. The time it takes to get there gives us ample time to set up the spike chains and so forth, ready for deployment. Worst case is the attack being called off for one reason or another right after kick-off."

And all these well-laid plans will change when the time comes. No battle plan ever survives the initial contact with the enemy, or so cadets are taught at West Point.

The Pursuit Preparation

Are we ready? Eagle asked. This is not the time to speak up. Everyone realizes that saying "yes" nails down high expectations, while saying "no" will release an avalanche of questions or chastisement or both. A measured response might be, "Are you fucking kidding me?. . . we know little more than nothing, so how can anyone claim to be ready?"

The screen on the back wall comes alive, thanks to the diligent efforts of an audio-visual technician who surfaces for a minute or two. A PowerPoint show—abysmal graphics, but clear and concise text—helps the attendees keep up with the presentation.

One of Eagle's underlings acts as a stand-in for Eagle, who's by now losing his voice. "Uniformed Security's visible activities should not change in volume or intensity.

167

No reason to offer clues that we are awake, is there? Vehicles patrolling the outside perimeter have been equipped with always-on video recording, so that the patrol need not slow down or show any kind of curiosity to traffic going in either direction. A team will scrutinize every frame of the videos when the patrol's shift ends. The standby SWAT team will make best efforts to remain invisible. We made arrangements for temporary housing, along the lines you would find in a fire station, with kitchen, showers, and bunk beds—TV should help alleviate boredom. Some snipers will be dispersed with the teams ready to set up the roadblocks; only a few will stay with the SWAT team."

A dialog evolves on how the roadblocks will be set up to look like a construction mishap. Lots of Road Narrows signs, orange cones, orange lane stripes, temporary concrete median dividers, big generators with construction lights, trucks with a huge load of gravel capable of blocking even a sizable truck. Hidden spike strips. Chase vehicles will face in both directions. Most visible workforce will be wearing orange coveralls; those hidden from view will be wearing camouflage uniforms. Traffic flow will be controlled by running a Bobcat in and out of traffic lanes to make sure that vehicles will pass the choke point at the desired speed, fast enough to keep the cars from bunching up, yet slow enough so that both overt and covert observers can get a good look at vehicle and occupants. Any car that looks even slightly suspicious will have a suitably charming individual, dressed as a private security guard, signal the driver to lower the windows for a chat and better opportunity to peek inside. To keep the atmosphere light and non-threatening a few lame jokes along the lines of "Any day now" and "the next porta-potty is three miles down the road...." will be offered.

"Covert security, meaning SWAT, snipers and heavy weapons will be hidden in a tractor-trailer, about a quarter-mile back from the choke point at the barrier. We will jack up the trailer and have one deflated wheel off and lying on the side of the road."

An invisible voice from the back of the darkened room pipes up: "Can you define heavy weapons?" Another unseen voice from the other side of the room clears the air by explaining that the term might have been misused. Linguistic overkill we learn. We are told that "We will have devices that can breach a lightly armored vehicle's outer skin with enough power to maim or kill humans but do minimal damage to equipment and cargo. Think oversized flash-bang grenade."

Which, of course, triggers the next question related to paramedic support: "EMT service staff will wait on the far side of the choke point, say maybe a mile or so away. Hidden in some way. Firefighters in the same spot. Armored vehicles as well. Anything that cannot be explained with a construction mishap we will hide."

Eagle's team has done a fine job planning.

"Air assets, the Broken Arrow team, the command post, and our press contact will be moved to or, if already there, stay at the National Guard Hangar at the Santa Fe airport. We don't have enough resources in that category to spread around."

The briefing continues for another forty-five minutes, and by then, we are beginning to lose the upper echelon—the grunts get to sit there and listen to the bitter end.

The Crooks Get the Huey

In the meantime, The Crooks had been busy. They left a voicemail on my cell. I did not listen to it until late in the evening after my final hop of the day. The content of the message was brief, and they asked me to call back "As soon as practical." I chose to interpret this to mean in the morning. The call, my trusted phone reveals, had been placed late in the day, while I had been consuming not one but two adult beverages to ease the pain in my neck from hanging out of the hole where the helicopter's door, which I left behind in the hangar, used to be.

I decide to call the customer of tomorrow's currently booked job and see what flexibility I could exploit once I follow up on the message. The farmer I am supposed to help find some horses that broke out of a coral about 36 hours ago never pays on time and the ongoing

171

pissing contest we have been cultivating will only increase in intensity when he finally realizes the meager chances of success. His land borders on a massive section of National Forest Service land, where, once hidden by the trees, the animals will be near impossible to track. We have been through this exercise before with buffalo. Since he never maintains his fences properly—because he is cheap—he now faces the prospect of paying me handsomely instead. Someone with a less onerous personality would be a dream customer, a gift that keeps on giving. However, the escapees were animals he stables and grazes for some car dealer's wife from Albuquerque, a true bitch who will cause real problems once it's clear that the horses are gone. I expect no flexibility in delaying the flight since delaying only further screws up the likelihood of success. But I try.

He answers on the eighth ring. I hear trucker music in the background, so he is home.

"It's Harry. Evening. About tomorrow morning: we still on?"

"Yep. Seven-thirty. I closed the barn door so you can land next to the truck. Don't shut down. I'll be there once I hear you coming over the hill."

No flexibility.

"Can do. Is there cell reception near the search area? Have to make a call when we land for you to have your smoke."

"I know all the spots with more than one bar."

"Alrighty then. Bring cash. It'll take two hours, after that the search area will grow too large. So, do I see three grand when I land?"

"No, you won't. I will make the owner pay for the search."

"You get paid to take care of them. Good luck with that. I don't have a stake in this; I get paid by the hour when the rotor turns – horse or no horse. Cash, ok?"

He whimpers and whines. I am tough as nails: I am on retainer by my new magic friends with the Huey AND with the Feds. In the end, I have a promise. I am the only game in town. It feels good to negotiate if the other side has no other options.

I take a shower. Alone. After the shower and the night that followed when Erin was here last, showering alone is pure agony. Zorro had been a keen observer of her creative instincts. I had tried to shush him out of the bedroom, but she had laughed and insisted that he might learn something useful, and he watched us, trying to decide if all the thrashing and moaning was in my best interest or a threat. I can report smart dogs are amazingly astute. Erin is traveling on business for a few days, so the best I can do is sniff her pillow for a faint whiff of her perfume. All I find is a fading residual hint of my Paco Rabanne aftershave. I quickly fall asleep.

Suddenly it's morning. I am tired of the tossing and decide to get up earlier than needed. Zorro and I share a breakfast, he gets a bowl of the kibbles he adores, and I get a bowl of granola with fruit. The two dishes are carefully selected to make him think that we are eating the same stuff; otherwise, I have to continually show proof that his is at least as good as mine.

I clean up, both myself and the kitchen, let the dog roam in the yard and throw some sweaty uniform shirts in the washing machine. There is a thin film of dust everywhere, proof that dusting is my main shortcoming as it relates to household chores. An SMS to the lady I occasionally employ to clean should take care of that.

I return the call from yesterday. It's six AM as I hit dial. After eight rings, the voicemail picks up.

"It's Harry. I realize it's a touch early, and I apologize. I am about to head out and will be flying probably till noon. I plan to land and stretch my legs about once an hour, and when I find a spot with decent reception, I'll call. If you have a specific time that is good for you or if you have a better number for me to call, please leave me a message, and I'll do my best to call then."

As soon as I hang up, the phone rings.

"Hi. Could not grab the call in time. Just listened to your message. Can we meet at the Huey, say 2 PM? Bring sectionals, old ones will do, so we can mark what we need doing. It's a photoshoot, and there will be six of us, so it's gotta be the Huey. We've assumed that you might want to take a look at the aircraft, fire her up and get light on the skids, check the maintenance log, all the stuff you aviators do. Will that work?"

Whoever is calling has a better understanding of helicopters and aviation in general than I am used to.

I decide not to ask for a check upfront this time since they will owe only pilot pay, not the operating cost of the Huey, and in the context of the overall relationship, I am willing to take a risk. Let's see if they bring the agreed-upon retainer without prompting.

"Can do. The gate code has changed. It's star 6273 pound. On the flight, will you be bringing equipment other than handheld cameras? And, please have all passengers step on a scale for me, will ya? Anything else I need to know?"

The response is no. I can't wait to find out what they are going to shoot and why it takes six guys to do that. Minor trepidations about being alone with six potentially hostile guys up in the air set in. Most of the time I rely on the fact that the pilot is considered a mandatory component of the flight, but here there are a whole bunch

174

of unknowns. The Feds are sure to listen to all this, so I don't bother to inform them of the pending flight. Furthermore, should The Crooks have tapped my phone or bugged my house, there is a good reason to play it safe.

I call for fuel for my Long Ranger and ask the desk to fill up the Huey since I have no idea when and where we will go scouting with the team that asked for the ride. Making the arranged time for finding the horses is getting tight. Zorro senses the urgency and lingers near the rear door of my car. I dump what I need onto the right front seat and blast off to the airport. A quick stop at the trailer is all I need to retrieve all that is required for the ranch job and the photoshoot.

It's just about seven now, and I fire up the Long Ranger, by now sitting on the ramp, a long way from the open hangar door. Nothing pisses off the crew charged with cleaning the hangar than a careless pilot blowing leaves, dust, and debris into the hangar, tightly packed with aircraft, wings intertwined and, therefore a bitch to broom. While I wait for the gauges to go to green, I listen to ATIS, converse with the tower, and proudly announce that I will defy gravity in the general direction of Truchas. They make me hold for an incoming American Airlines Bombardier from Dallas. The moment I hear his reversers come on, I lift into a low hover and am given a go to start heading north.

Twenty minutes outside Santa Fe airspace, I start descending and point the nose towards the barn of my customer. I do the pickup, make sure that the seatbelts are not dangling on the outside as I am keen to protect the expensive paint job that has already been ruined twice by some nitwit. When you are doing 120 knots, a belt buckle banging against the outside of the door will do a number on the paint. When one is wearing noise canceling headsets, the dings cannot be heard. For just about two hours I fly a search grid, making sure that the general area I am searching is chosen by my esteemed customer so that the

175

blame for a failed search will rest with the rancher, the horses, and Not With Me. After the three grand, now in my zipped pocket, are gone, he angrily admits failure, and I drop him off without shutting down.

I decide that I will probably never hear from him again. A brief review of this morning can be summed up with ". . . I had low expectations and I was not disappointed."

Blue Corn Café on Rodeo serves an excellent Tostada salad in plenty of time for me to saunter back to the airport. I tie down the rotor blades, ask for a tow back into the hangar and start walking over to the Huey. Then I am off to my lunch.

In reality, it's a Bell 205A++, a much better aircraft than what came back from the Vietnam war. Better engine, better maintenance; the Hobbs meter, visible through the closed door shows relatively low hours. A slow walk-around reveals little that I am not enamored with, no leaks, the doors are tight, the tail rotor has no play. I get a ladder and climb up to check the Swashplate, rotor head, blade attachments, I peek into the rear of the engine, and low and behold there actually is an engine in there. Having dealt with my paranoia, the next stop is my trailer since I don't have a key to the Huey.

Two o'clock sharp, I hear a shiny black Ford Expedition SUV pull up next to the Huey. Two guys I had not met before get out, they see me coming over the ramp and offer polite greetings. A key is passed to me, and I slide back the rear door for them to look inside, and I open the left front door. This aircraft can be flown from either seat and has the bulging bubble window for the external load work I so despise.

"Let me turn on the power and take a look for a minute, then let's talk about your needs."

A nod from the driver is all the response I get. Not the chatty type. When the battery comes on, the needles start to swing, and the humming of the old fashioned instruments lovingly referred to as steam gauge's make me feel comfortable and ancient. A beautiful new GPS from Garmin, the same one I have in my Bell 206, is the only really modern piece of avionic equipment.

Silent Stranger peeks past my knees and observes what I am up to.

"If you don't mind, I will take home the maintenance records tonight and make sure all is as required. So, let us chat about your mission, shall we? You wanted to mark up a map: let's do that in my office where there is space to unfold a sectional."

I leave the aircraft unlocked, and we go to the trailer. Zorro is introduced to the visitors and retreats to his worn pillow. My introduction is intended to reveal to my observant dog that, for the moment, all is good, but that these are not friends, they are customers, not to be growled at—not to be cuddled either. And, should they turn hostile, you, my dear Zorro, are free to maul them.

"When and where do you need to go, for how long, how many stops, etc.?" I inquire.

It gets interesting in a hurry; they plan to fly around quite a bit—the same general area where we did the photoshoot with the girls, up the Pajarito mountain and over into the Caldera. That cannot be a coincidence. Right outside the Lab's restricted airspace. For the time being, I withhold comment.

We agree that two days later, we will depart with six plus pilot and full fuel for what might be a two to two-and one-half hour flight. No cargo. Open the sliding doors in the back, front doors installed. I get an envelope in exchange for a handshake. They take off in the Ford.

177

I go back out to the aircraft once they have left, take a perfunctory peek at the records and fire her up. Nothing out of the ordinary. While the temperatures creep towards the green, I leaf through the maintenance records. Nice and clean, with text printed on adhesive labels and all endorsements signed and dated with the associated Hobbs times. The first thing I notice in the records is that there has been a series of installations and removals of optional equipment done just a few weeks ago, with virtually no flight time in between. It also appears that a few recent ADs, as in Airworthiness Directives, have been complied with.

The temps are normal now, and I crank up the power and lift her into a low hover. The needles go to where they are expected; all the annunciators are out. I land and shut down. Nice safe aircraft.

I decide that the rest of my thinking and planning might as well take place at home. Zorro needs a walk and a fresh bowl of water before we blast off towards my humble abode. I stop to pick up my favorite microwave dinner: Mary Calendar's Beef Pot Pie and a bottle of Jack Daniels. To stay competitive, waistline wise, I skip the bucket of ice cream.

During a stop on the drive home, I call Eagle's assistant from a payphone at a gas station and divulge the afternoon's outcome. Eagle himself must have been listening in, kind of sneaky, and predicts that my potential willingness to cut corners and risk minor infractions will be tested during the flight.

I see his point: I am being cultivated for something—the story I was fed does not really hold up. Eagle is keen to find out what they have in store for me; my curiosity is dampened somewhat since Eagle's ass will safely be in a comfortable office chair while mine will be out there to face the music.

The Command Post

The camper arrived via the pass that separates the Valle Caldera from the Los Alamos plateau. The spot where Deputy Chris's blood pool has long since dried up, as has the possibility of re-settling the camper in the same spot. The campground at Bandelier is busier this time around.

The spot where this camper had previously stood is now occupied by a family with three kids and two dogs, reason enough to seek another place, away from the noise of the kids and the sharp instincts of the dogs. It turns out that at the spot chosen, the noise from the kids is replaced with the noise from the occasional passing car or truck. The two guys, who earlier had so abruptly ended Chris's life, go about the tasks of setting up their camp with the dexterity earned by a dozen practice sessions at various campgrounds in Northern New Mexico.

The most unusual piece of camping gear that emerges from the cargo bay is a communications package bristling with antennas. For proper security, a bumper sticker, stating that the owner is a member of the ARRL, the National Association for Radio Amateurs, hints at the antenna's purpose. A good deal of pulling and tugging helps, and it finally arrives at its place on the roof of the camper.

The towed dingy is disconnected from the RV and parked facing the exit of the campground. The food for the virtual dog stays hidden inside this time; there is good reason to offer no enticement to the dogs of the neighboring family. After that is taken care of, the two retreat into the interior of the camper, leaving the outside as clean and orderly as any decent nature-lover would want it to be. The image of the model gentlemen camper lost some of its shine when they fired up the generator, but with no one within earshot, not a cause for chastisement.

The feeling of this campground visit, as opposed to the one a few weeks ago for scouting, feels a lot tenser. The tone between the two and the tone of the radio chatter differs significantly. Every effort is made on the radio to create a dialogue that implies that someone is trying to unscrew a screwed-up situation. Packages on the wrong truck, lost paperwork, missed messages. The tone between our two, on the other hand, is clearly affected by the sense of closing in on the mission; their tone is brisker, snappier, articulated more crisply.

Jose shows up in due time to hang the camera drones near TA-55. The plan had gone through some modifications after extensive testing revealed a tricky problem due to the propellers' whining noise; sneaking in these drones undetected required more background noise to camouflage their arrival than had been measured during rush hour when half the Lab left at the same time. Some fairly creative thinking led to a solution: fly the drones to the power line alongside the road some distance away from the gate, hook onto the top cable, and using a low power setting slide them along the wire to the intended position. This neat trick allows for getting the eyes of the team into position without the need to stick to rush hour. And it will allow for a ground vehicle to be dispatched if a crashed drone needs to be retrieved. Just positioning the drones, a mandatory item on the project checklist, is in itself quite an operation, but Jose has it covered. When he's done he'll head to the campground, even though he knows he will be early. That is the plan.

The moment the door of the camper opens and Jose steps inside, an encrypted SMS arrives, stating that "All times have been moved up 45 minutes. We have inside info on the schedule of the shift changes. Both for installing the drones and for the actual operation, the shift change offers a brief time window when the gate area remains unmanned and security is maintained through remote operated cameras and sensors. Their's—not our's."

John is intrigued. "How did we get that shift schedule?" Jose somewhat reluctantly states that, as usual, sex had a lot to do with it. "How so?" an intrigued John wants to know." One of the guards, supposedly happily married, is diligently screwing the blond waitress he met at the local watering hole. Their affair, currently in its steamiest phase, requires careful coordination to stay active. And thus the shift schedule, a classified document, was shared—and the most recent paper copy came up for sale. She is not the sharpest knife in the drawer. Reminds me a lot of the joke "How do you make the eyes of a blond sparkle? Shine a flashlight in her ear."

The operation goes down smooth as silk. A few minutes before the shift change, a biker shows up pushing his bike, evidently because of a broken chain, past the gate area. It is his hushed voice that triggers the drone placement. By the time the new guard team shows up, eight minutes later, three small drones are hanging near the gate, offering overlapping, unobstructed views of TA-55.

Ready to Commit Arson

We fly the Huey. The flight is uneventful. To me, it remains totally unclear what is going on: they can't square the story I am being told with what I observe. John sitting in the co-seat asks for the passenger audio to be isolated. Okay, now the two of us can chat with no disruptions, but I can't hear what's going on in the rear. We scoot low over the Caldera as if looking for elk. I have a hot tip for them: the elk disappear in the trees once the sun comes up. So, it's not elk we are looking for, are we? Neither do we have an explanation of why we go study the Pajarito Mountain Ski resort. It closes after Easter if they are lucky enough to have snow still then. It's almost summer now. Too late for skiing—and too early for hikers.

We turn south.

And then, it turns out, Eagle was right.

"Let's go back to the shot location down on the river." Been waiting for that.

"I have to go a little to the left or the right from here; otherwise, we clip the restricted area."

Give him a chance to reveal himself. Wait, Waiiiiit—wait. Just a little longer.

And here it is: "Don't tell me that anybody is watching this desolate piece of half-burned down forest." Gotcha. What comes next: a solicitation for a criminal act? *It is illegal, without prior authorization by the controlling agency, to enter an area that has been designated as restricted airspace. The use of deadly force is authorized.* It says so on the map.

The time for me to show a cooperative attitude (and earn my keep) has come. "I see. Let me descend towards Los Alamos Airport, and then turn right a bit. The guy at the Los Alamos airport that drives either the fuel truck or the fire truck, depending on what the moment calls for, is the first guy the Lab will contact, if at all. He knows me, they know me. It's gonna be cool." I have just delivered proof that I am willing and able to break the law. Just a little, but, this is important, break—not bend.

After some additional useless dicking around, we head back to Santa Fe Airport. The return trip provides an opportunity to determine what's next.

Coughs often indicates that one is about to hear a fictional story.

John coughs twice and then pops the question.

"You may have noticed the Firestarter in the back? The AIDS?"

I did. "I did."

"We have a contract with the Forest Service to burn some old brush growth. Something you would be willing and able to take care of?"

I have to point and lead this in the correct direction, so I respond, "That job would be part of our standby agreement?" Always come across as a bit greedy, a sentiment that comes natural to me. It turns out it is part of the agreement. "When and where? How many acres? Will I have spotters on board?" I need to either not do this job or get rid of the spotter. The AIDS can be operated from the pilot seat.

"There will be three of us on board. Spotter, AIDS operator and you."

No, there won't.

I decide to milk some more info while the going is good. "Can you mark the sectional with the area to be protected?"

He squints at me. I do not want to display any ulterior motive for asking questions. I diligently wait a few seconds and then look at him to see if he heard the question. He did. The time has come to save the day.

".... or will the Forest Service provide the coordinate list, as usual, at the last second, too late to do a weight and balance?" The squint stops.

I land. We jointly decide that my mechanic will look at the installation instructions for the AIDS and do the paperwork. Once that is done, my cherished clients and I will later fly out over Lake Abiquiu and fire a few rounds off, to demonstrate that all is well.

Everybody seems to be in a hurry to get out of here, and so I wait for the gate to close behind them. I proceed to the FBO office, where I borrow the landline phone that is explicitly, in strong language, reserved for calls to Flight Service for weather info and then I call The Eagle. This phone line should still be ok with no one listening in.

Again, some assistant answers. He doesn't recognize the caller ID, and therefore I am subjected to a most aggravating minute of Q and A as to Who I Am, and what the reason for my call might be. I am subjected to Federally approved Hold-Music till Eagle comes online.

"What's up?"

"Here is the *Reader's Digest* version. We took up the Huey. We were hanging around the perimeters of the Lab. Great efforts were made to make it look innocent. They claim that they are under contract to the Forest Service people—I don't believe a word of it—and they want the AIDS mounted to do a prescribed burn." I know that the Forest Service would never let an unfamiliar civilian contractor go on a prescribed burn by themselves, so this story is pure fiction.

A short pause at the other end. The background noise on the phone goes silent for a few seconds—clearly, there is a whole group listening to the call—and then he is back with "Alright. Let us stick to the plan. Once they trigger their project you make sure that the Huey is disabled. That should put a dent in their plans." This seems a bit too hasty/wishful thinking for my taste since they could well have a backup plan we haven't figured out yet; as a matter of fact, we still know very little about what is going on here. I wish I could be joining Eagle's team during planning sessions, yet we all consider this too risky in case I am being followed.

Ready for the Escape?

The Crooks had purchased two large, essentially new RVs along with a collection of elderly sedans, SUVs and trucks. The first RV was already parked at the Bandelier campground a while back and it was manned and equipped as the operations command post. Now it is back in the same campground. The timing called for the command post to be abandoned in one hell of a hurry once the heist had been successful. It is to be cleaned of fingerprints and DNA residue, and set on fire while the ops team descended down the ravine to the river. Or the plan could change to proceed down Route Four to Bernalillo, if that seems preferable from a timing viewpoint.

The second camper is larger than the command post and had been a few hours ago parked at the Tetilla Peak campground right off Lake Cochiti. Rather than towing a smaller car, this motor home here is a toy-hauler, containing three fairly substantial inflatable boats. Two are meant to be used, one is earmarked as a spare. Careful research had shown that not only was the camp underused during work days, but this campground has a boat ramp. The Rio Grande, navigable only with inflatable Zodiacs, flows into Lake Cochiti. The plan calls for this second RV to be on standby to dispatch and receive the ops team, who on return will abandon and sink their Zodiacs at the ramp, move the team and the yield of the break-in into LANL to the camper, and take off southeast bound.

The genius of the plot was to leave a large SUV parked under a highway overpass with the intention of moving the stolen goods, and later the proceeds of their sale, while the RV would be abandoned some distance away, close to where the escape vehicles for those team members no longer needed had been stationed. Always have a backup plan.

Now the time has come to find a fire truck.

The Tesuque municipal fire station is operated by volunteers, and it is mostly unattended. Due to its proximity to Santa Fe and Pojoaque, both of which have permanently and professionally crewed fire stations, the Tesuque station relies on Santa Fe's men and equipment to get to a fire much faster than calling up their own marginally trained and poorly equipped amateurs. Therefore, the Tesuque Fire and Rescue is the obvious target for obtaining trucks and uniforms.

The gravel parking lot across from the fire station just outside the village center offers a marvelous vantage point for checking the comings and goings at the firehouse. And that was where Todd had two guys monitoring for any potential problems in setting up and executing a raid. The cover used in this instance was, ingeniously simple and effective, to get the two observers camouflaged as bikers. A good deal of effort for local flavor and authenticity went into this: from wonderfully light titanium bikes, tight-fitting bikers' pants, glossy shirts only a biker would wear, leather gloves and day-glow red helmets. But the one idea they were most proud of was to make the chain jump the gear "on request" so that both could stop anywhere and fiddle for as long as needed with no further explanation required if challenged for some strange reason.

The instructions given to the observers are "Hang around the Tesuque Village center, check what is the routine around that area. Take some pictures. Be invisible."

Three days of part-time monitoring revealed that there were two aging, but functional, smallish fire trucks parked in the garage. On the second day, someone showed up for five minutes to handle what looked like a battery change on something not discernable in the dark. On his way out, the light in the garage came on for a few seconds. It revealed an abundant supply of generators, spare hoses, extinguishers, but, more importantly, uniform pants folded over the boots and jackets, helmets, and gloves hanging on the wall. Everything that is needed to show up at a fire incident looking like you belong. On the third day, a quick trip past the garage door, ostensibly to dump some trash in a container mere feet away, delivered proof that the lock would readily yield to a single blow with a sledgehammer if needed.

And just then, when it was really called for, an unexpected gift presented itself. At the very instant, when the observation was deemed over, a Toyota that had seen better days shows up, a man gets out, leaving the engine running and retrieves the key from a lockbox; a lockbox flimsy enough to yield to any sizable screwdriver. The Toyota departs quickly after dropping off some paperwork. Now it is painfully clear that the sledgehammer is just a backup, the key from the lockbox being a lot less noisy to retrieve. It actually should have been pretty evident that a key, accessible with a code, is an excellent solution under the circumstances.

The idea is to wait till the last minute, then break the door and drive the larger of the two trucks out, while the other team members helped themselves to uniforms. The plot then called for departing rapidly in the wrong direction "....to confuse the Russians" heading southbound on US285, away from Los Alamos. The raid should be over in less than four or five minutes.

Assault

The Magician David Copperfield uses misdirection by giving his audience a shiny object to focus on, while the lady that was placed in the wooden box to be skewered with swords slips out behind the curtain. Works every time.

Buying Amtrak tickets one-way from Raton, New Mexico to Chicago, purposely using a credit card that had earlier been used to charge for drinks back in Santa Fe's watering holes and therefore presumably known to the Feds will serve as the first source of misdirection. The general idea is to offer ample opportunity to chase the robbers in the wrong direction. Nobody is going to Chicago. Just about everybody will head south.

Many team members, mostly the complete planning team, have now departed and scattered in all directions. Anyone not needed on site anymore is gone.

Staff meetings have been replaced with re-arranged video conferences via VPN.

Team members have all been told to toss all used burner phones, replace them with new, virgin "burner" phones. At a thousand dollars, apiece the term burner hurts. Using brand new iPhones is just not justifiable, and so the revised strategy is to pre-arrange video conference calls, using FedEx computer rental by the hour. Everyone has been instructed to shred all paperwork and have those replaced with encrypted PDFs on the new phones. New encryption keys and new passwords have been installed on the phones.

Todd, just before kick-off, passes out a list and goes over mandatory or go/no-go items, events that must occur for the final go, when the point of no return has been reached. Also listed are those that must NOT occur—the kill items. He goes over timelines, maps, contingency plans. After the keys of parked escape vehicles are distributed, everyone, nervous and uncertain when and where the next assured meal is going to come within reach, enjoys some fine catering. On the way out, all are going back to their rooms to wipe off all fingerprints, and polish away much of the DNA left behind. Just inside the exit door of the meeting room waits a box with night vision goggles.

Todd and his two assistants carefully watch the departing group to search for any hint that somebody is about to fall apart.

Zero hour is midnight. The roll-call over text messages, precisely at 2355 hours, shows up, and they get a "Phase One is a Go." It's pitch black outside, the rationale behind the night vision goggles, and it just started to drizzle. Drizzle is good: reduced, yet not obstructed visibility will help. The automatic weather reporting at the airports in Santa Fe and Los Alamos reveal ceilings about 500 feet above the terrain. The Huey can handle that. So can the pilot.

Todd heads to Lake Cochiti, where he will monitor progress. His lieutenants are all heading to their assigned posts. Jose will join the RV at Bandelier; Mike will head up the team that will play the roles of the firefighters, while John is joining Todd and the rest of the assault team to launch the Zodiacs and head up the river.

Loading the assault team with all their gear into the minivan is done in a jiffy. The minivan was bought way back in Amarillo, and the Texas plates exchanged with New Mexico plates. The van has been dinged and scratched all over by the previous owner, a landscaping business. It looks beaten up, but it is roadworthy, and it looks just like the original from the actual shuttle service that departs from the bus stop on Cerrillos Road. The self-adhesive stickers imply that this van is now being operated between Santa Fe and Chihuahua, a few of hours south of the border, where just about half of the Mexicans that work in Santa Fe are from. On the way from Texas, a low spot on a wet dirt road did provide the kind of dirty patina that makes the vehicles legend credible.

The drive from Santa Fe to Lake Cochiti is planned to take about 45 minutes in zero traffic. In this weather and at this late hour, when no one would ever consider sending a retiree outside, near zero traffic is expected. It takes all of 35 minutes, although the speed limit is being adhered to with almost painful diligence, this not being the time to get pulled over for blasting down the roads.

The van stops short of the campground, and one man is dispatched to quietly scout for any unplanned observers. At last check, the extraction RV stood almost alone. A quick examination now reveals that one of the two vehicles seen here two days ago is now gone. The remaining other camper is up on blocks, it looks dirty, and its entry door is obstructed by a collection of enough tumbleweed to conclude that it is at least temporarily abandoned. One item on the kill list, lack of privacy during the launch, has been eliminated.

To head from the campground up the river at night in this weather at this hour calls for black wetsuits and night vision goggles since lights on the lake and on the river would be out of the ordinary. On the other side of the lake is yet another campground that has been proven to be more popular, being close to the Pueblo's center; even in this very dim light, a few tents are visible due to the bright orange fabric of their outer shell. Anyone getting up to pee outside in this ungodly weather would immediately notice lit boats being launched. Suspicion might follow.

The equipment bags with weapons, infrared lights, radios, bolt cutters, and ropes for the descent down the ravine had already been distributed among the inflatable boats.

Once the camper is locked up, and everyone checked over, an exchange of SMSs solicits a Go signal for the next sequence of events. The response takes longer than anticipated, generating some minor anxiety that evaporates the moment a reply dings on the team's phones.

Under the team leader's breath, whispered instructions are issued, even though during numerous rehearsals, what needs to be done, by whom, and when has been pounded into the head of each team member. They like to call themselves "the Marines," yet when you hopelessly search for them in near-zero visibility, "Seals" would have been more appropriate.

Todd and John are sitting in the darkened camper and watch the activities outside, keeping their fingers crossed that noise be avoided. The fully inflated Zodiacs

194

are dragged out of the toy-hauler compartment, down the extended ramp. The van departs, heading towards a parking lot at the Albuquerque airport.

Todd turns to John and asks, "Ready?"

John Chavez is a careful fellow, who survived two tours in Afghanistan in the service and one tour as a Blackwater contractor with not a single injury, so he takes a good fifteen seconds scrutinizing the progress made outside and finally responds with a terse "Ready."

Todd takes a deep breath and says, "Then go. I'll be here when you get back. If not, disband the team, abandon all the stuff we brought here, have everyone grab their bag and make a run for it. Good luck." Abort procedures had been discussed in great detail among the cadre, yet that part of the plan had been diligently withheld from the grunts. No reason to introduce new doubts and hesitation to a team that, in an earlier life, always had an enormous backup team. The United States Military does not send people into harm's way without a plan to jump in and save their necks. No such cushion is available tonight.

John steps outside. The others gather around him, sitting on the sandy ground between the two Zodiacs. He crouches down to their level as well and offers, "We are good to launch. Four men to an inflatable. Don't drop the bloody things." He waits for questions. "Questions?" None forthcoming. "Let's hit the river then."

Like ghosts, Todd hears the Zodiacs fade into the darkness, long after the black-clad humans who barely remained visible have evaporated into the dark.

Todd is used to the task of being the commander. And he knows that waiting away from the action is the most challenging part of command responsibility. It's lonely at the top. For the next several hours, he is stuck listening to the radio, hoping that it will remain silent, as all relevant interactions of the others will be via text message. Any radio traffic would signal bad news.

Inaudible mumbling one's thoughts is a way to hide the anxiety that all leaders face, once the troops have been committed to battle.

He remembers his ROTC teaching assistants summing up his views on leadership with ". . . if you are a leader and no one is following you, then you are just out for a walk."

First doubts and questions seep into Todd's thoughts. How come it took so long to get the go-ahead? Why the hell did I decide to stay with the assault team instead of going with the fire brigade? Or drive to the other campground? Now all the decision-making responsibility is with the guys at the campground, and I am down here with the sole task of waiting for the goods to arrive.

Let's Steal the Fire Truck

It's twenty-two minutes after midnight, and the objective for the fireman's team is to block the small road between Tesuque Village Market and the I285 ramp for the duration of the raid. The most worrisome potential issues are barking dogs, curious insomniac neighbors, and bad luck. A real fire alarm would screw things up royally, but the likelihood of that happening right now is pretty remote. A decision has been made to respond if queried, that the roadblock is due to a (fake) gas leak.

Mike is driving up I285 to raid the Tesuque Fire Station. Six of his guys are crunched up in the back of a vehicle, way too small for the mission, partly because the car also holds traffic cones and detour signs. And a sledgehammer. The drive is over almost immediately. At the bottom of the southern Tesuque exit ramp, an extremely brief stop disgorges two guys, dressed as volunteer firemen on traffic duty wearing the obligatory reflective vests, for not more than a few seconds, the signs directing any traffic right up the entrance ramp, back up onto the highway. Nobody expects such a roadblock to be manned at this time, and in this weather—drizzling rain. A spike strip behind the detour signs and traffic cones does not invite violators and would undoubtedly stop anyone drunk enough to run the gauntlet.

The fire equipment storage facility, maybe a quarter mile down the village road, is surrounded by some residential housing, previously verified to house no animals that represent a threat. House cats and hamsters one can choose to ignore; dogs would be another story. The most impoverished New Mexicans, many owning nothing of value, often seem to own pitbulls with the nastiest personalities. The wet weather will probably drive them inside anyway.

The team's vehicle proceeds quickly past the Fire Station to set up the second roadblock in the center of the village, right before the only grocery shop and sandwich place in the village. Same procedure as before: traffic cones, a detour sign, a spike strip. And off they go, heading back the couple of hundred feet, where the driver pulls off the road in the southbound direction.

Silently the car arrives in the gravel parking lot; the two that will always be classified as the Muscle get out, one with the industrial size screwdriver, the other with the sledgehammer, and within seconds the small lockbox holding the key is open. The taller of the two leaves behind the sledgehammer and heads for the main circuit breaker on the backside of the building, just in case the lights are wired to come on automatically upon entry. Both doors slide up slowly, gently, and with little, if any, noise. Now the rest of the team emerges from the waiting car, they dash across the dark and lonely road and run into the building. Everything happens quickly, the cables that connect the battery charger are pulled while deft hands load uniforms, and all the other items on the shopping list are tossed into the back of the fire truck. The theft is over and done with by 12:35. Thirteen minutes, start to finish, is two minutes short of the schedule. It had been previously agreed upon to abandon the detour signage, the spike strips, and burglary tools in place. No reason to care about the confusion that will undoubtedly confront the few early commuters as to why they are forced to make a lengthy detour with no discernable cause.

The designated staging area is the public parking opposite the Camel Rock Casino. Are there issues with that choice? The threats and problems are the casino's video surveillance, their alert floor security as well as the suspicious old sheriffs' deputies that protect the parking lot of the casino. They are unlikely to pay much attention to the public parking that's devoid of any vehicles in the middle of the night. The drizzle seems to have let up a bit.

Mike is keenly aware that he and his team have ample time to drive carefully over and up the hill to Los Alamos. The guy in the right seat asks, "Want the flashing lights? Sirens?" No, you idiot, I want to create as little attention as possible. "No, let us keep it quiet till we get the message that the fires have been set. And they will be set once the team that has to crawl up Frijoles Canyon, in the middle of the rain and at night, is in position."

It takes only a few minutes to get the firefighting equipment from Tesuque on the collector lane to the Camel Rock viewing area, even though the convoy, for security reasons, had initially been heading in the wrong direction.

From the back of the fire truck that Mike is driving, he hears a distant voice asking, "If we are heading to Los Alamos, how come we are going south?"

Now Mike is pissed off, both angry and disappointed that all the past briefings and project meetings did not seem clear to all the participants, and his response articulates that disappointment as he raises his voice and shouts, "Because we are trying to confuse the Russians. Why am I burdened with morons?" No one offers an opinion, in part because none was solicited. And no one knew precisely and for sure, which moron he meant. Everyone is tense. Mike is forgiven.

The ramp where the interstate ends and Saint Francis Road begins, all of four minutes after they left Tesuque, offers a convenient and discrete option to turn around and head north again. "Someone, please verify that we are alone." The fellow sitting behind Mike offers that there is not a vehicle in sight. Sometimes cops follow emergency service vehicles simply because that might save time. Adding a sheriff's car to the convoy would not be convenient right now. Ten minutes later, they arrive at Camel Rock.

Upon reaching the parking lot, Mike shuts down the engine, checks that the driver of the other vehicle is following his lead after that truck has slid up next to his vehicle. Mike turns around and says, "Ok, let's get out as silently and with as little light as possible and get dressed for the part."

Mike hears the rear doors open, and he senses bodies sliding out of their seats. He checks his phone for texts. No messages. Good news. Not even fifteen minutes later, everybody is dressed and back in the truck. "Smoke them if you have them." Now comes the boring, the stressful part: waiting.

Harry Sabotages the Huey

When I get a call in the middle of the night, it sometimes takes me a minute to wake up to that point where what is being said sinks in. I have learned that taking notes while I listen is my best defense. A pad, a pencil, and a light await such calls and mess up my nightstand. The ring tone I have elected to use would wake up a hibernating bear, a feature needed when walking around a noisy airport or when the ring must fight the ding of a noisy bar.

The phone must have been ringing for a while before I was able to grab it, not yet clear in my head, failing to look at the screen. The sound that came out of my mouth might have belonged to an angry crow rather than a half-asleep aviator.

In a hoarse voice, I managed to say, "Hooooose zis?" It was Mike. I had been warned to expect a call via an earlier text message. Back when that call came in, I was surprised to realize that it was only 8:30 pm and it was then that fog in my brain cleared and I realized that the quick nap after the evening news turned into a deep sleep. Zorro was lying on his side at the foot of my bed; by the time I managed to raise myself off the bed and turn on the nightlight, he opened one eye to monitor my actions. Satisfied that all was well, he went back to sleep.

Mike rattled on: "Can we meet at the Huey? We have a job to do. Say in an hour? It's important. I'll pay the usual rate and a fifty percent bonus for the short notice. I'll explain." What the hell is this? The Huey was all set up to do the controlled burn we had discussed, so what do these guys want at this hour?

On tomorrow's schedule is a long list of minor housekeeping tasks such as ordering supplies, billing and paying bills—no flying, nothing that couldn't wait. So I suggested that we meet at my airport office; I had no desire to talk out on the ramp in the dark.

That was thirty minutes ago, and now I am awake and standing under a shower cold enough to make me awake, angry, and wildly speculating what this newest twist in the story could mean. Do I have time to call the airport and get the weather? A quick peek through the shower curtains promises shitty weather. I will listen to the weather on my phone in the car. Do I have time to call the Feds before I leave my house? What do I tell them? I decide to wait to talk to the Feds after I learned the reason for this surprise call.

As I approach the gate to enter the ramp, I see a black Ford ahead of me pull up to the gate, and an arm emerges from the driver's window to enter the gate code on the keypad. I sneak through the gate right behind before it has a chance to close. Both vehicles park directly outside my camper. I am out first and open the camper door to get everyone out of the drizzle.

As soon as the lights are on and we all are squeezing into the narrow space of my cluttered office I take a moment to check the appearance of my customers, and it becomes apparent that they have planned to be outside in the rough and the wet; their boots, pants, and parka are from Carhartt, I can see the labels. Another mystery: they are not dressed for a ride in a helicopter, more like lumberjacks or miners.

There is no right way to express my disdain for dragging me here, and I open up the dialog with "Evening. Why are we here?" The nameless fellow I recognize as one of the lieutenants offers, "We decided to do the controlled burn tonight." I hold up my hand and inquire, "What made you decide to go fly around in the middle of the night in shitty weather?" The nameless lieutenant's lack of coherent response surprises me: ". . . Todd talked to the Forest Service, and they believe that the rain will ensure that the controlled burn stays controlled." Shades of the time when said Forest Service burned down half of the town of Los Alamos and a good portion of the Lab, when that particular controlled burn got away from them, cross my mind.

I have no intention of complying with their request. Actually, I am more than surprised, I am concerned. It dawns on me that I agreed to take care of this and that I am on a retainer, specifically to assure my availability when called for. Simply refusing to fly might lead to me being reminded of my obligations in less than friendly terms. I am also keenly aware that I have yet another agreement, this one with the Lab, to look out for relevant developments and report back. Logic dictates that this flight must be part of a more substantial undertaking, yet I can't see an opportunity to send a text message or make the urgent phone call that Eagle is paying me for.

Making an impassive face is not easy. I decide to go along until I find a plausible way to back out of my predicament.

I turn and offer, "Alright, it's your funeral. You aren't going to like the ride. You will get cold and nauseous. I have barf bags in every seat pocket. Since we are in the Huey tonight, you will miss my best punchline: On my bags in the Long Ranger, on the inside bottom, it says, 'Thank you for flying with Santa Fe Helicopters.' Back when I had them printed, I thought that was hilarious. No one who had to make use of them thought it was funny. Let's go over to the Huey and get organized."

I am handed a piece of paper with all of the waypoints for the flight. No way to determine where this route leads until the data is in the GPS.

The lieutenant and I walk over to the Huey while the others park their vehicle; I leave mine sitting next to my office.

I unlock the doors, I climb in, fire up the avionics, and start to enter the waypoints, and the map display comes alive. I am blown away: now I can guess what they are up to—and have no good way to alert the intended victim. I feel boxed in. If I decline to fly tonight, I might be seen as a 'removable' obstacle; if I do fly, I might later have the full clout of the Federal agencies come down on me. It feels like having been invited to dinner, for the same evening, by Jeffrey Dahmer and by Hannibal Lecter, neither being a desirable choice.

I do know, however, how to at least get my rear end out of my predicament. I turn off the master switch, mumble under my breath what a shitty idea it is to go set fires in the middle of a rainstorm, and inform my passenger that I will now perform a preflight check. Climbing up to the roof of the Huey allows me to open the engine cover. When my body is positioned such that my observer cannot see my hands, I swiftly loosen the nut that connects the ambient air going to the fuel control, knowing from experience that this will keep the engine from developing full power. And that will kill the flight. I smile reassuringly, button up the engine cover and climb down from the roof.

"Whenever you are ready." By now, all the passengers are back, they climb in, and I rattle off my standard briefing. My hands fly over the switches; all is well, and I hit the starter, wait for the RPM to come up, and introduce fuel. I am being observed carefully as I do a full runup.

"Everybody strapped in and on the intercom?" I hear the expected responses and crank up towards full power. Except that my little treachery works as intended.

I point to the gauges and say, more to myself than anyone else, "Not coming to full power. What's up?" No comments. I lower the collective and then raise it back up. Of course, I get the same results. I fiddle for visual effect with switches, I tap my knuckle on the glass of the offending instruments, lower the power again. It is a remarkable acting performance. I turn to the fellow in the passenger seat next to me and proclaim with fake disappointment in my voice. "Hate to tell you, but we ain't going nowhere tonight."

I can see that this is not welcome news. A sense of mistrust is palpable by now since they can't tell if I am the cause or the victim of this problem. I turn and explain that I cannot get full power and demonstrate the problem. "Let's shut down and decide what the next steps are."

Once we are outside the team, other than the lieutenant, scatters. They make frantic phone calls and send urgent text messages. A phone is handed to my front-seat passenger, and a brief conversation ensues, of which I can hear only one side. I hear a lot of yes's, some no's, the expected four-letter words called for at this juncture. The call ends with "Will do."

They look at each other, then at me, unable to determine if they are being screwed. The tension is thick.

There is more than a controlled burn at stake here, but now I can begin to piece together what is going on here. These sinister characters are planning to set fire to the Lab.

I had not expected the next question, "Can we use the Long Ranger instead"?

No, we bloody well cannot. I quickly realize that this is my opening for withdrawal. "No, the mounting bracket for the Long Ranger is very different and won't fit. How about tomorrow? Can we do this tomorrow? The hangar is locked, and all the tools to check out the problem with the Huey are inside. The mechanic that works for me shows up at eight-thirty earliest. And the least I need from him is a signature." Everyone shakes their head in disgust. I inform them that I'm going to go home to ponder my options, and I promise to call first thing once I know what the problem is. I turn and drag my helmet and the flight bag back to the camper and lock up. No one stops me. I climb in my car and head out of the gate, leaving the whole bunch, wet to the skin by now, standing next to the Huey making phone calls.

Just as soon as I am on the road leaving the airport perimeter, I call my contact number at the Lab, and because no one is there answering the call—your tax dollar at work—I leave a message for an urgent callback.

Geronimo

The Crooks fear is that the whole plan for the heist is coming apart at the seams. The text messages previously exchanged between them are evidence that the project is well underway: The Zodiacs were launched, and on their way up the river, the fire truck is at its standby position, thirty-five minutes away from gate 55; the drones that are showing the gate's activities in a green infrared image are in place, and the escape vehicles are in position. All that is needed now are the two fires, the one at the heliport as the distraction and the one near gate 55—the one for the heist.

At this moment, the fire setting equipment mounted on a helicopter that has been declared grounded due to equipment problems or what airlines like to call "operational reasons."

So, what is a crook to do? Call the whole show off? And then, unable to repay the money borrowed in Los

Mochis, run like hell before an angry drug lord comes chasing after every single member of the heist team? Antagonize the elderly, elegant Mexican gentlemen behind the entry door at the Hacienda in Los Mochis? A hasty exchange of text messages reveals that no unified response to the challenge is forthcoming. This not being a democracy, a stern reminder from Todd that "It is I Who makes The Decisions" shuts the nonsense down.

It takes not more than a few seconds after that message when Mike's phone rings. It's Todd.

"Can you take the AIDS off the Huey and put it on a truck?" Todd's voice is calm, and he has found just the right tone of authority. Mike considers how to respond and comes back with, "We have an elderly green Ford 1500, in the dark difficult to distinguish from a Forest Service vehicle, parked at Lowe's. No more than fifteen minutes away."

"Can you get the AIDS off the Huey and put it in the bed of the truck in such a way that it is operable? And can you do that in time to be there at two?" Mike assumes that *there* means at the gate.

That requires some thinking as well, and after a brief pause, Mike replies, "We can get the Firestarter off, likely with few minor problems. We don't have the proper tools, but it might work. Mounting it might work with tie-down straps, and we have plenty of those. But if we manage to do all that, there is no way to test the functionality. I can't set the airport on fire, simply to test if it works?"

Todd has a clever solution for that and says, "You can test with the glycerin injection turned off—all we need to know is if it spits out the rounds, on fire or not. And make sure to collect them all, we don't want to leave more clues than necessary."

Todd comes back quickly with "Let's proceed like that. Give me a text message update every fifteen minutes. Out."

Mike sends one of the guys in the Ford to Lowe's to pick up the truck. The rest of the group, wet, angry and uncertain swarm over the helicopter, disconnects the power, pulls the wiring harness with the controller and the mechanism off, and starts hunting for something to put in the back of the green truck tall enough to make the burning rounds clear the walls of the vehicles rear rather than set the truck's rear on fire. Behind one of the hangars, a plastic bottle crate is retrieved that will, when turned upside down, function as a table for the AIDS. Crude, but functional? Only a test can tell.

After a lot of pacing back and forth by the group, the green truck shows up. Eager to try the installation, since time is of the essence, the group snaps to work.

To everyone's surprise, the kludge worked. If this were not a moment of high stress, high-fives would be called for. Not tonight.

At one-thirty sharp, a text goes to Todd with the feverishly anticipated words: "Ready. Say when." Mike knows from the timetable and some quick math that if he is to leave the airport, no longer by air, at the same time the firefighting team departs the parking lot, they will all arrive at the same time. Just about at two a.m.

Two fires: one at the Lab's helipad to disable the choppers, and to take out the Lab's firefighting equipment. The other one at Gate 55.

Mike's math is dazzlingly accurate: after leaving Pojoaque and heading towards the road to Los Alamos, the green Forest Service lookalike and the Tesuque fire trucks end up driving right behind each other. The weather has deteriorated as the night rolls on, the ceiling is now five hundred feet, and the rain had steadily increased again over that last hour. Flying would be difficult now, so the problems with the Huey were a blessing in disguise. Mike remembers that Harry told him that nighttime flying is when bad decisions and stupidity tend to punish offenders instantly.

The convoy splits up, the green truck arrives just short of the heliport, just inside the perimeter of the Lab, right on time. The fire truck hangs back a quarter mile or so and waits for orders. A broadcast message goes out, demanding a status report. Clearly, everyone has been glued to their cell phones. Cochiti is a go, Bandelier is a go, Zodiacs are a go. If it were audible, this would sound like a NASA launch countdown. The magic word flashes on the screens, and the magic word is *Geronimo*.

A few seconds later, the truck with the arson team heads up the road. It passes the fence outside the gate, mere feet away from the hangars and the storage facilities, where all the Lab's emergency service vehicles are hidden in the darkness. The truck slowly passes it target, and someone's finger presses the trigger on the AIDS device, which flings little white balls over the fence. They land a few feet apart and promptly burst into flames. The maintenance crews of the emergency base, usually bored stiff due to lack of activity, had done a great job removing grass and brush, leaving little fuel and, therefore, a disappointing, meek trail of fire. Mike is not worried and says to the others, "Give it time."

As the truck speeds up and heads towards the actual target, away from the distraction, the equipment pinched from Tesuque follows at a distance. Once it is clear that the fire, given a few minutes, will reach the structures at the base, a confirmation message goes out to the group. As Mike speeds up to catch up with the arson team, he observes in the rear view mirror the first few substantial tree crowns bursting into flames. As he turns the first curve, he sees the smoky, orange embers from the crowns of the Pinions jump from tree to tree. He knows that in a few minutes, there will not be much equipment left.

It is no different when the lead vehicle arrives at gate 55. Same procedure, same result. Here the fire spreads much more quickly; here, there are caretakers with better things to do, other than to remove shrubs and grass. Once the vehicle reaches the end of its journey, backs up, and for good measure does another pass, the word goes out that this step too has been accomplished. As soon as there is some distance separating the truck from the fire, the AIDS gizmo is tossed into the bushes.

Ian to the Rescue

On my way back to my home from the airport, I think about what just occurred with The Crooks and the Huey. What do I know, what do I suspect, what actions do I take?

I know that The Crooks are up to no good: too many inconsistencies, too many wrong signals. I know from the waypoints that there was an attempt underway to set fire to the perimeter of the Lab. I know from the timing of the aborted attempt that this is not a Forest Service contract job. I know that the Lab is as of yet unaware of that attempt—no one called me back yet. No reason to panic: no one, other than me, can fly the Huey tonight.

I suspect that The Crooks realize that I potentially have enough info to piece together what they are up to. And I feel an urgent need to find a way to improve my

213

personal security. I suspect that the fire is a diversion, part of a criminal undertaking, rather than sending a message. I suspect that the rest of the individuals involved in this, those that I had met or observed, are still around somewhere. Thus I suspect that I am aware of only a fraction of the big picture.

I decide to call the Lab again, and raise all kinds of hell, either by explaining to a live human being what happened or leave yet another message with a great deal more urgency. And I will need to get some help. Time to call Ian.

Ian is about as thrilled to get a phone call after midnight as I was. He wakes up a lot quicker than I did. At this point, I am no longer sure what I had told him and Erin back when I asked for help, should I ever ask for assistance. So he gets the *Reader's Digest* version, strictly about tonight's events. I have no desire to try to outline my interpretation of all the pieces of the puzzle I am confronted with—too much time would be wasted. Ian wouldn't care for the fine print anyway.

So I ask, "Ian, I need your help. Meet me at my house as quickly as possible. Bring pepper spray and a gun. Zip-ties if you have them."

He is one smart cookie and perceptive as hell. No questions, he just listens. I hang up. Not more than ten minutes after I slithered into my parking space at home, he does the same. I manage to make yet another call to my contact at the Lab. It is the answering machine again. How the hell am I supposed to help the Feds if no one is ever home?

Ian is dressed like anyone who gets a call like that in the middle of the night. He is wearing shoes, jeans and a shirt, no jacket. He is wet like a man who had to run through the rain to get to his car.

I give him a quick rundown, and tell him, "This is likely a hazardous situation."

He responds calmly with a terse, "I got it."

I continue with, "I left the group back at the airport. I was apologetic about the trouble with the Huey, with a casual attitude, like a guy who can't wait to go back to bed, and in no hurry. My concern is that despite the fine acting, that I might be viewed as a risk to their operation. I tried to talk to the Lab again; whoever is supposed to minding the store is not picking up. I need to be able to tell the Lab, should they ever return my fucking phone calls, about what these guys are up to now. Questions?" None forthcoming.

Now comes the tricky part as I ask, "Would you please go back to the airport and check what the hell is going on? If I show up again, that will raise all kinds of alarms. Check if they are they still there? If so, hang around out of sight and follow them once they leave. Be bloody careful, they are pretty sharp. Remember the gate code? Leave the car outside and walk through the man gate, not the one for the vehicles."

He gets up and heads towards the door. As he exits, I yell after him to take my parka, the one with the hoody, that is dripping water in the entry. The dark swallows him, and I hear his car start and depart, spraying my screen door with gravel.

Mike Crashes the Gate

The bigger of the two fire trucks, the one on loan from Tesuque, has vertical bars across the front bumper. Useful for pushing cars to the side of the road and to crash through gates and other obstacles. The outer fence of the Lab has an entrance whose job is to keep casual visitors out. It is separated from the solid barrier with huge concrete median dividers to zigzag through, by fifty feet. For anyone who had traveled to East Berlin during the cold war will remember the look and feel of Checkpoint Charlie.

Mike knows from the last update that the vehicle with the Pit is now parked in that area. Since the van is carrying only one Pit heading to Amarillo for testing, the big rig and the escort vehicles will not be needed: it will be just one white van driving to Texas. This information is derived from the transport schedule, leaked by the girlfriend of the guard, and from the imagery that is coming in from the drones suspended near the gate.

Nothing is moving. The realization that the trees are on fire, not just at the helipad, but here as well, hasn't filtered through the system yet. That will take a few minutes longer. Since the Lab's emergency equipment is stored at the helipad, everyone alerted will use the inside perimeter road to rush there. The group in the truck has grown by one individual from the Zodiac team, picked up minutes ago; the rest are hiding in the bushes, recovering from the climb up the ravine.

Mike sits in the driver's seat of the fire truck. Total silence engulfs the inside of the vehicle. He's waiting on the main road, close enough for to see the outer gate, but he stopped far enough back to be invisible from the inevitable security cameras. The tricky plan is to pick up enough speed to crash through the gate yet make it look like an accident, not an attack. Not easy, but it can be done.

Mike does it, near perfect. He accelerates up the road on the left side, speeds up to a frightening pace, swerves right and hits the swing gate in the wire fence, breaking right through. "Piece of cake," someone mutters. The truck hasn't stopped yet when they jump out of the vehicle right at the moment when the driver of the minivan with the nuke pops out of his car. The driver has, until a few seconds ago, desperately been trying to report the fire emergency. One would have expected him to have seen the phase when the fire was set, but he had his head down sitting in the windowless dispatch office, doing paperwork, however, when the green truck did its job.

The whole thing is over in a few seconds and the group gets to work. The first one out of the truck uses a Taser on the driver. They zip tie him up, drag him to a spot on the ground with no grass, only inflammable gravel. The big guy, soaking wet from sweat and the rain, with the crowbar rips open the back of the minivan. The open door shows but one box, the size of a small suitcase, no markings. It is holding the Pit. Mike is standing well back, observing the transfer of the case into the back of the green truck. Mike yells, "Clear?" and he hears lots of "Clears" but no "Holds." A lit Molotov cocktail is tossed into the back of the Lab's van, right back where the spare gas container is, and a second bottle hits the front compartment. The inferno that erupts engulfs the vehicle completely. Mike climbs in, taps the roof through the open window, and yells, "Go."

The brief stop where the rest of the Zodiac team is hidden in the bushes to transfer the stolen case goes off without a hitch. Mike's team proceeds to join the team about to descend the ravine with the loot.

The fire truck and the green truck are incinerated and abandoned, some distance away from the ravine. Good luck finding prints or DNA in the ashes, are Mike's thoughts as he joins the others.

The steep descent through Frijoles canyon is slow, tedious, and interrupted by falls and crashes. The group is larger now, and therefore slower. Mike's trusted Lieutenant gets to play tail and ushers two stragglers along. Everyone ends up caked in mud. The ropes that had been left on the trail, back during the ascent, help for navigating the unmarked trail. The tall, dark trees, presenting a challenge on the way up, now call for a brighter color rope. The rope does little to provide for a smooth descent. The line chosen for that task is too thin; it had been selected based on the requirement for minimal weight and bulk to drag up the ravine. It does not provide enough friction for the wet and muddy gloves, and the descent takes a lot longer than anticipated. And time is of the essence.

Mike knows that they will emerge down at the river exactly where the photo shoot had taken place. Out of breath, he watches as the case holding its prized possession is loaded into the boat. The inflatables, freed from being tied to a tree, drift, and spin in the water as the Zo-diacs head down the river towards Lake Cochiti.

Each inflatable carries two engines: a small, fast, noisy two-cycle Honda and a slow, noiseless electric pusher. The Hondas help by making up for the time lost in the descent, as the dawn is no longer far away. A dia-logue is neither called for nor is it possible with the little two-cycle engines screaming their little hearts out. Once the last curve of the river is approaching, the gas out-boards are shut off, and the electric motors are lowered into the stream. The active campground on the other side of Lake Cochiti might come alive early, so they need to be quiet.

Both dinghies follow the center of the river, mere feet apart. Barely audible, Mike checks around. "Any inju-ries? Anything left behind? Anything lost during the de-scent? All radios off or on low volume?" He counts the thumbs-up signaling that, while some tools and equip-ment have indeed been abandoned, everything left behind will intentionally direct the pursuers towards a wild goose chase. Casually abandoned old boarding passes and res-taurant receipts give false evidence: the city of Toronto re-emerges as having some ill-defined role in this drama.

Right below the campground holding the RV is the boat ramp, and the two boats follow the GPS pointer and sneak up until the bow touches the concrete incline. Eve-ryone exits, and they jointly drag the case up the slope. The last man off the second Zodiac points, first one and then the other boat back towards the mouth of the river. A quick slice with a bowie knife along both sides lets the air out so fast that the boats begin to fill with water just in time for the last man to jump onto dry land. The battery-driven propellers are on and will guarantee that the boats will sink to the bottom of Lake Cochiti, a suitable distance from the shore. The snowmelt is underway, bringing a lot of muddy water, so spotting the dark rubber boats from the surface is impossible. It will take a diver to find them.

Being found is expected, but much later, at a time when all involved assume that they will be sunburned, emitting clouds of Margarita vapor at a distant beach.

Todd's Most Prized Possession

Todd is proud of himself. Up to a point. He knows damn well that in the annals of criminal behavior of the blackmail kind, the moment of exchange is where the ice is thinnest. All preparations for that exchange are risky as well. Up to now, they have been mostly lucky. The mess with the Huey he had not been prepared for. The fact that Harry came back to the airport while his team was fitting the fire-spitting gizmo to the truck, he was not prepared for. It was by pure chance that Harry's green parka was spotted just before the dark swallowed him. The need to dispatch potential witnesses like Harry he had been prepared for. Everything else went smooth as silk.

The next steps are based on some assumptions. One of the more significant risks was that the Lab was onto them and rigged the case holding the Pit with a booby trap. Todd calls out, "John, take the case outside, put the Pit on a picnic table, then tie down the unlocked case on the table. Do all this no less than a hundred feet away from here. Use a rope to lift the cover while ducking behind a mound. And do all this with no light, while not making a fucking sound."

John wished that someone—anyone—else be charged with that task. He squints, hesitates, gets out, and does as instructed. The case opens—no booby trap.

High on the list is defeating the tracking device that may or may not be embedded in the case. In a moment of sheer brilliance, Todd had asked, two weeks ago, that the huge storage compartment in the back of the RV be lined with aluminum foil, creating a Faraday cage which would disable a suspected tracker. Not only are the raiders worried about a tracker in the case with the Pit, but also that one or more could later be mixed in later with the money. Todd had gone over that part of the plan in great detail, to ensure that those with the lesser intellects could follow. Men hired as muscle rarely are familiar with the finer points of physics.

It is still dark, but dawn rears its ugly head in the East. Everyone is packed up and ready to go. Todd says, "Move forward a hundred feet" to the driver and then calls the team together to go over the ground foot by foot to check for left-behind items that might betray their heritage through DNA or fingerprints. All is well.

Still clad in wetsuits, all board the camper. At near idle, the camper creeps forward and departs the campground. County Road 16 leads back via uninhabited Pueblo lands, towards the interstate. The ten-minute drive is over soon, and as the interstate comes into view, everyone is in khaki pants and short sleeve shirts. Only the driver and front seat passenger are discernable, the others are well hidden in the bunk beds, invisible from the outside.

Todd is in the front passenger seat and keeps a sharp lookout. As the ramp to the interstate approaches, he reminds the driver to head for the northbound ramp towards Santa Fe. As they come up the steep incline called La Bajada where the terrain flattens out, the driver spots the roadblock at a commercial inspection station that has not been used in a long time. He shrieks, "A fucking roadblock! What the hell do we do now?"

Todd's head jerks up; he sees the sea of red and blue blinking lights. "Slow down, even slower, let me think." An option to turn around before reaching the roadblock does not exist. The queue southbound is short, no big surprise at this hour. He counts four pairs of headlights shining in his direction. No brake lights on the northbound side. His voice is low and calm, and he says, "That's the turn off for County Road 57; the one we will take. It runs along the railroad tracks towards Cerrillos." He pauses. Everyone in the back is holding their breath. Todd's face lights up with a chortle, and he says, much louder now, "This is great. They are looking for anyone coming FROM Santa Fe, and we are going TOWARDS Santa Fe. They will wave us right through. Once we are past the checkpoint, we are home free."

The mood has changed from exuberant to tense; the word from behind Todd is that "There are no atheists in a foxhole."

Ever slower, they creep up the highway towards the exit, towards the cops. There are lots of vehicles standing around. Some of the cars are positioned past the actual checkpoint, past the laid out but folded spike strips, trucks in green and camouflage paint. Not well-hidden on the other side of the road, Todd spots an armored personnel carrier. As he peers past the southbound vehicles, the drivers being interrogated, he spots bright dayglow orange traffic cones and guys in white helmets and orange safety vests.

He turns his head sideways and around and says, "Smart. These guys are not stupid. A roadblock made up to look like a traffic collision or a construction accident. Not bad. Could have been my idea. Everyone will remain invisible. Do it now."

Todd reminds the driver to go really slow, keep the windows closed, ". . . but look in their direction, like any normal nitwit gawker going past police activities. You are a natural." This insult goes right over the driver's head. A state trooper standing in the center of the lane steps aside and waves the camper on with a "no gawking here" hand gesture. In a few seconds, they are past the congestion and on County Road 57. Everyone exhales.

At first, the road is paved, but a few miles in it turns into a well-maintained gravel road. As they continue, the trail gets narrower, bumpier, full of potholes. As they drive parallel to the railroad tracks, a steep and very tight little pass has to be negotiated.

The Sangre de Cristo foothills have ghost towns or underpopulated tiny towns about to go dormant littered everywhere. Remnants of a thriving mining industry back in the late eighteen-hundreds, back when Cerrillos was a town with twenty-plus saloons and brothels. Now it's a sleepy little place, sometimes used as a movie set. On the outside of what looks like a stone barn, an observant or curious traveler will learn that Lillie Langtry, a British actress and opera star, had performed here. So, the miners back then could choose between opera and brothel?

As our friends are driving, just before reaching Cerrillos, they pass through Waldo. There is literally nothing left of the once busy town. Behind the railroad track, one can just barely spot the ovens, now falling apart, where ore was once processed and then shipped out. Right behind the main track, which carries the Southwest Chief Amtrak, twice a day, between Chicago and Los Angeles, are some rusty old spur tracks. The nearest two train stations in either direction are Lamy and Albuquerque. Other than a few Railrunner shuttles between Albuquerque and Santa Fe and the occasional freight train, not much moves on these tracks. As they drive past the ovens of Waldo, Todd's thumb points to the pullout next to the tracks and some huge cottonwood trees, and he informs the group that "This is where we will come to pick up the money."

As if called for in the script, all those present display a lustful grin. There's that vision with the tanned surfer babes and the cocktails, umbrella included, flashing before their collective eyes again.

On the outskirts of Cerrillos, they join the old road to Albuquerque. Free of any interruptions, their drive takes them to the Hyatt. An online reservation made weeks ago, in a false name matching the credit card, is waiting for them. No one has any intention of making actual use of the room, and it's too early for a check-in anyway. The room reservation is for later in the week. This does allow Todd to drop the case off, now covered in a canvas bag, holding this prized possession, with the comment that the guest will pick it up upon check-in. A nice young man with a name tag marking him as the bellboy hands a receipt for the bag to Todd and holds the door open for Todd's departure.

Now Ian is Missing as Well

They did it. And I was too dense to see it coming. And so was the Lab.

The story of the fire is all over the national news and totally swamps the local newscasts. I am glued to the television with 9/11 intensity. While I know little, my knowledge of what happened is far broader than that of the Talking Heads. Considering how little info is released by the federal and the local government, much of the news coverage is competent, thoughtful, and reasonably accurate. Some of it just awful, mostly speculative, and the journalistic competence of the reporting seems at this point to be determined by the individual journalist rather than the editorial standards of the broadcast network or station. There is no getting away from it, even at seven in the morning.

My cell phone spent the night resting on the wireless charger right next to my pillow, not a sound all night long. I keep checking my text messages: not a word from Ian. I conclude that the activities at the airport must have stopped by the time he got there.

So, they found a way to set a fire. No one is aware of any involvement of mine; I expect this blissful status to end soon. Nowadays, leaks are a question of *when* not *if*. On the spur of the moment, I decide to add a deadbolt, today, to the front and back entrance— "for my security and comfort" in airline lingo. There is much to be said about instincts.

As Zorro has been pacing left and right inside the screen door, I decide to let him out while I prepare his morning bowl. The drizzle has stopped, yet he is back shortly, the patch of ground he recognizes as his bathroom is covered in six-inch wet grass. Now I have a measure of how long a jiffy is. He is well aware that climbing on the sofa with a wet belly is frowned upon. I congratulate him on his perceptiveness. He lies down on an old piece of shag carpet, one eye closed, one eye on the bowl.

I am fighting the coffee machine, dressed in shorts, a no-longer clean t-shirt, and loafers, when I hear and see police cars pull up, blue lights—no siren, blocking my driveway. As I pull back the curtain on the kitchen window, I count one Sheriff, one State Police, and one city cop in marked vehicles, followed by a dark grey SUV with no official markings and no hubcaps but a lot of antennas. The room darkens as five bodies block the light coming through the glass door at the entry. I hear the doorbell. I pick up my mug, unlock the door, hang on to my mug with both hands to show how unconcerned they should be, and open the door. Zorro is at my side and pokes his head out through the partially open door.

No one from the small posse wanders to the back of the house, so I conclude it's not me that they are looking for. None of this "Ring the front doorbell but watch the backdoor" stuff.

I smile and offer, "Good morning. What can I do for you?" to no one in particular, trying to figure out who will speak first. I follow that with "Don't worry about Zorro here."

A guy in a dark grey herringbone suit, Hispanic facial features, blessed with polished manners steps forward. Always send in the infantry first, I suppose. He scrutinizes me from head to toe, coughs, and says, "We'd like to talk to Harry Anderson."

I offer, "That would be me. To what do I owe the honor?"

He repeats, "We'd like to talk to you."

I step aside and hold the door open, and with a wordless hand wave invite them in. We remain standing in the small, crowded entry.

"Do you know an Ian Larson?"

And I reply, "I sure do. Why?"

The Sheriff's Deputy, a short, intense guy who must work out daily, stands there, legs apart, and asks, "Where were you last night between midnight and four?"

Without hesitation, I say, "Here—the whole time. To save time: no, no one can vouch for that. The only witness is Zorro here. But tell me: what has Ian been up to, in order to justify such an impressive show of force?"

State patrol now remembers that he has a speaking part in this scene and says, "We took your driver's license from his pocket?" Now I remember having placed my driver's license in my parka, the parka that Ian wore on his way out the door. I am confused by the choice of words. "Took" seems like an odd term.

"Is Ian being questioned, and what for?" I ask.

Herringbone, friendly yet firm, says, "We will get to that later. When did you see him last?" It is as if we are rehearsing a scene from a Bosch episode.

"He was here around midnight, we had a brief chat, and he left. It was raining pretty good, and he was dressed for different weather, so I offered him my parka. I had worn the parka earlier when I went to the airport, and my driver's license was in the parka's pocket."

Next comes "What is your relationship with Mister Larson?"

"We have been friends for a long time. Met him in the mid-nineties. We have an occasional meal and or beer together."

"Do you own a .22 caliber weapon?"

I get it: Ian must have shot somebody. I am getting a bit concerned now and decide to take great care to be very precise in my answers. Although they must have looked up the relevant records and already know the answer, I say, "I own a twelve-gauge shotgun, a .45 SIG pistol, and two .357 Magnum revolvers. No .22s; never owned one. Neither does Ian, at least as far as I know." They do already know that. That was just to test my truthfulness.

This is when I learn that Ian is dead. Found sitting in his car, shot with three rounds of the .22 caliber. Two shots to the chest and one to the head. The shots fired through the closed car window. An execution: Only professionals use .22s. This caliber has a low muzzle velocity, is easily silenced, and the soft lead bullet expands to a massive size on impact. Great murder weapon at short range. I sent him to his death. The bastards must have looked at the parka, possibly with the hood up, and thought it was me.

Shock, surprise, despair are my most dominant and spontaneous thoughts: I am not used to losing friends, other than through aircraft accidents.

I am told that no good explanation as to what he was up to has emerged, even after the State Trooper found pepper spray, a bunch of industrial size zip ties, and a small caliber revolver in Ian's car.

Anger, rage, fury that I was up to now unaware I had the capacity for, wells up in me. Some quick thinking is called for: Tell them nothing but the truth, but not the whole truth. There will come a time when I'll have figured out who the guilty parties are. There will come a time when I figure out what to do about it. But right now, I need to project shock, surprise, and sorrow. I do not find that difficult. To gain some time, I open the screen door to a confused Zorro who remembers his last pee break mere minutes ago and looks at me with bewildered eyes. I follow him out the door with an apologetic "Zorro needs to go outside. Be right back." While the dog makes useless efforts at yet another pee, I pace back and forth in sweaty anger.

Back inside, my next question is, "Where did you find him?"

An early riser walking her dog near the near San Ildefonso Pueblo stumbled over him in the Bosque. Her dog had dragged her there. She then called the Pueblo cop, I learn. Ian must have followed them and got caught. They haven't figured out yet that his dead body is connected to the fire, but they will.

A lot more questions follow. I am faced with a delicate dance: evasive answers might move me from the witness category to suspect. Forthright answers will violate the security agreement in place. Such disclosures will also become an obstacle once I decided what to do about my friend's murder.

It's time to clear things up, but stay well within the constraints of the security commitment I had made, and I tell them, "I just watched some news. This homicide is peripherally connected to the fire at the Lab. I have signed a non-disclosure agreement with the Feds, related to work I did for the Lab, and I can't say much for that reason. I would like you to contact Matt Murphy, the resident FBI agent at the Lab for more info. I expect he will listen to you and then brief me as to what I can say and what not."

Now, this, as opposed to the extent of my gun collection, comes as a surprise to them. The Sheriff's Deputy, short and perpetually angry like many short people, is just about to get in my face when Herringbone holds out this arm to silence him and says, "Thanks for the update. We will be back."

I bet you will.

It takes no more than an hour after the cops left for Matt to call back on my residential phone. I consider myself to be a peripheral figure in what I suspect is a much bigger mess than the fire that I learned about on the news. I spend an hour soul searching and putting together the few puzzle pieces I have seen.

Let's summarize: I had worked for a bunch of crooks. Mike wanted to use the Huey to set fire to the Lab. Why we don't know. Yet. I defeated that part of the plan by disabling the Huey. I went home. Left a message at the Lab. Mike found another way to set the planned fire. Ian must have followed. In the dark they thought it was me again, wearing the same parka as before. Ian's efforts were misinterpreted as Harry's efforts, making me/him a witness with too much information. The cops figured out that I know more, I just about admitted that much.

The phone rings. I pick up and recognize Matt's out of breath voice saying in one continuous stream, "Finally listened to your voice mails from last night. Got a call from city and state fuzz about the body they found. Sorry about your friend. Utter chaos here. It's more complicated than just the fire. What did you tell them?"

Sorry about your friend? No compassion, just sorry?

"I answered their questions. Just the facts, nothing speculative. I told them to call you. Tell me: what's more complicated than just the fire?"

Matt is silent, probably pondering how much he can reveal. He says, "The fires were a distraction. They were after something they then stole in the raid at the Lab. Something we want back. This last part is classified. We are trying to keep a lid on this breach."

I suppose he won't tell me what the raid was all about.

He continues with "We are looking for them. We put up road blocks everywhere. Too late of course. They dumped the vehicles used in the raid along the way. All burned to a crisp or clean as an operating room, therefore no DNA, no prints, no business cards. Nada. We are still looking. But we know what they look like, thanks to you." The frustration in his voice is palpable. "This morning we got a text message from Toronto. Meaning from a phone with a Toronto area code, the call's ping showing up at ORD in Chicago. Offering, listen to this, to sell us back what they took. Cojones the size of bowling balls. Did you hear from them?"

He must not have paid close attention to whoever called him about Ian. "Nothing. They believe that I am dead." An image of him slapping his forehead flashes by. "Some uniform from State Police will show up to continue the questioning. Should be there in half an hour. You home?"

You called my landline. Must be the stress. "Yep."

He wants to wrap this up. "He will bring along a release for you to talk to him about what you know about Ian and his involvement. Talk about your customer relationship. Not a word about anything else. You have worked for us in the past. That will explain the NDA. If I can get it done in time, someone from our Albuquerque office, a civilian, will join you. Need to run."

Let's Add ISIS to the Mix

One of the new office buildings, not yet ready for occupation, but ready enough to be confiscated and configured as a crisis command center, is crawling with humans. The Lab continues to grow in terms of workforce and projects all the time, so Eagle grabbed the empty space nearest to his office. The entry doors are not installed yet, so an imposing figure from the uniformed security group is checking badges.

Two distinctly different characters make up this particular cast: earnest, disciplined, mid-career, mostly men, are dragging filing cabinets, temporary office furniture, all manner of communications and computer gear into the room. One guy, standing erect on a stool, directs the traffic in a scene reminiscent of the Omaha Beach Landing on D-Day. Most members of that group wear blue or black windbreakers with the name of the department they work for stenciled in big, bright yellow letters on their backs. Setting up crisis management command centers is all they ever do. And they are good at it. Been there, done that. Calm, efficient, self-confident. They even bring their own huge garbage bins to collect the packing materials. All dialogue is subdued, no yelling across the room here.

The second group differs: they stand around, some helpless, clearly, outside of their comfort zone, some wearing traditional, dark, office garb. These would be the admin and security people. The third group, many in casual-Friday cargo pants and golf shirts—are scientists and engineers of the elevated pay-grade that tolerates such heresy. The golf shirts will be the group that answers technical questions. Most, if not all, decisions will be made by blue windbreakers, the decisions blessed by those in sharply pressed suits.

In the back of the room, facing away from the desk, folding chairs are set up in a precise, semi-circular layout facing a screen. A hastily fired up projector insists that the briefing will begin at 10:00 a.m. sharp. Bring a pen. No electronics. Leave your cells in the bin at the doorframe. Handouts will be waiting on the chairs, the screen promises.

It is now ten to ten. Eagle and his entourage come up the stairs. A brief verbal exchange between Eagle and his lieutenants ends with one gray-haired suit replacing the guy directing traffic on the footstool. The piercing whistle with two fingers turns all heads, the room goes quiet, and he instructs that it's ten minutes before the kick-off for the meeting, only yellow badges allowed, so everyone else "Get the hell out. Do stay in proximity to the building, do not talk among yourselves, be on standby to answer questions, and or make suggestions or proposals. Yellow badges find a chair. All others, no exceptions, leave right now. Dismissed." The Eagle nods: "Nice job."

There are a lot more chairs than yellow badges. Seats are filled in clusters, the grouping determined either by agency affiliation or by past working relationships.

Eagle prides himself in his ability to instill a sense of joint discipline among a herd of different species. As the time reaches 9:59, an analog clock projected on the screen ticks down to ten sharp.

"Welcome. We set aside thirty minutes for a kickoff meeting. Let us set the scene for you."

He looks around. All are seated. All wear the proper badge. Most of them he knows.

"Al? Al, please stand up—Al here will be giving the overview briefing. Please hold your questions. Al?"

Al gets up and replaces Eagle at the front. He grabs a Laser pointer. Everyone who's been in one of his briefings knows that he habitually uses Lasers to point at the audience, rather than at the screen.

"Morning. Early this morning a group of individuals, group size not established at this time, set two fires at the Lab's perimeter, as a distraction for a penetration of the secure perimeter near Tech Area fifty-five. The penetration was not anticipated, although we had some advance warning that activities directed against our interests were underway. We were even aware that fire might be involved; however, we were not aware of any plan to invade the Lab. Our expectation was that anti-nukers would try to create an event to embarrass us, to create news, to rally their followers. Wrong: they wanted a Pit. They got a W-88 Pit. We had a dummy ready for substitution; alas, the raid took place before a switch could be made."

Al, and Eagle, standing right behind him, can barely hide their embarrassment. The look on the faces of the novice participants manifests their surprise. The collective recognition of having been caught flat-footed is hard to swallow.

Al continues, "To add to our problems, we intercepted a message, badly encrypted, from an unfamiliar cellphone to an ISIS recruiter whose communications we monitor. The message offers, in pretty plain words, for sale one new, not refurbished, PU-239 Pit from a W-88 warhead. For a moment, let us assume that no one knows about our efforts to intercept communications. This then means that the raid was done by freelancers with no existing order for this item. So, for the moment, let us not handcuff and beat up every dark-skinned, unshaven individual wearing a checkered rag on his head. Middle-Eastern terrorists may well have had nothing to do with this. If, on the other hand, the author knows or assumes that we monitor that traffic, then the message was in reality directed towards us. Trying to create a bidding war."

Eagle signals his approval by not interrupting.

"We have roadblocks on all major roads, using concentric nested circles, one roughly 5 miles out, the other 30 miles out. Map with their locations coming up. Can I have that map, how about *now*, time is of the essence for fuck's sake, please? So here we have the location on Highway 4 at the Caldera, a second one at the turnoff to Cuba, also Highway 4 where it joins the road to Pojoaque, then on Interstate 25 just south of Santa Fe on top of La Bajada. Also on 25 going north at Glorieta Pass. Inside this outer ring we tow every parked car that looks abandoned."

Al fidgets in discomfort, whereas Eagle is pretending to take notes, his head down to avoid eye contact.

"We suspect that a camper that had been sitting at the Bandelier campground was their command center. It's gone. A fire truck from the Tesuque volunteers, stolen just before the raid, was used to crash through the gate. Abandoned. State police found a body of a Caucasian male. No

240

indication of a connection yet, but the timing coincidence is suspicious. All cell phones we had been monitoring went silent and invisible, last pings around ten last night. That's it for the moment. We will form groups with specific responsibilities. After the Q and A, please remain seated to receive your assignments and meeting schedule. Questions?"

Bitcoin or Cash?

Eagle sits in the office he had requisitioned at the National Guard Hangar at the Santa Fe airport. Outside is an aide on the phone, on hold, holding up his right thumb at the three o'clock position, signaling that he is waiting for the requested callee to come online.

Eagle hears, "Thank you, Madam Secretary, he will be right with you."

The thumb comes up; Eagle picks up the receiver and says, "Good morning Madam Secretary. I have been asked to give you this, your second briefing, as to where matters stand in Los Alamos. This was current as of about thirty minutes ago. I am ready to respond to interruptions at any time. I will confine my update to new knowledge acquired since the initial briefing. First of all: we received

243

a text communication from someone claiming to negotiate on behalf of the thieves. The message came from a rental PC in a FedEx Office location in Chicago. The store's security video system does not cover the computer stations, so that's a dead end. The brief message offers the return of the Pit in exchange for a large amount of cash. The Pit's serial number reveals that this is the real deal; the number could only have come off the device. They ask for cash: used twenties and fifties, as confiscated, drug money, random numbers, one million dollars per suitcase. Total twenty-five suitcases. At first, we were surprised by their modesty; when you look at weight and volume however, this makes sense. I would be surprised if they do not have a verification method in mind to counteract the use of counterfeit bills.

It is obvious why Bitcoin was not requested; it is most difficult to turn an illegal asset into untraceable used bills, useful in daily life, so asking for old drug money skips a lot of risky steps. We are given twenty-four hours to respond with an ad in the contact section of the *Chicago Tribune*. "Mid-fifties, white heterosexual male, based in Illinois, seeks to find companionship and love, marriage not excluded." They are not asking for anything other than an acknowledgment and a contact cell phone number. We are developing options. Currently, we propose and are actively planning for a three-prong approach. First of all, the FBI, supported by State and Local law enforcement, will investigate this as any regular burglary would. Follow the evidence, interview witnesses, the usual. Second, we prepare the money and come up with tracking methods, in anticipation of an exchange. Third, we monitor on a broad basis, all regional electronic communications, including but not limited to the usual suspects. Our strategy will be to get the nuclear device back, at all costs. We can chase the money and The Crooks later. This completes my briefing, Madam Secretary. Do you have questions for me at this time?"

She does not.

The Exchange Planning

Much of Todd's team has dispersed in all directions. The planners and research staff had started to head out and away days before the raid began. What's left is the core group, the members of which "shall be compensated by a percentage of the project bottom line." Meaning One Suitcase Per Person. The others are on a time and material type contract. They will be paid later. Probably. Maybe. For sure. A substantial chunk of the haul will end up going back to Los Mochis, back to where the startup seed capital had come from. Back to the gentle old man, sitting at the desk behind the door, while his assistant credibly played the role of the drug lord? If there is one thing Todd learned while supervising the shipment of cocaine through the tunnels under the border it is to "Never cheat a drug baron."

VRBO is a great organization. They rent furnished housing, mostly by the week, typically by absentee landlords. The rent is prepaid. The key "can the found in a lockbox in the carport." No one ever sees the landlord or the caretaker. Perfect. The property Todd had arranged for is located in the foothills of Albuquerque, just off Tramway. The stay was paid for with a pre-paid gift debit card. A quiet residential neighborhood with upscale housing. The van marked as the Chihuahua Shuttle is parked at the airport in the overflow parking for shuttle vans. Excellent security, yet no undue scrutiny.

By now, everyone has moved in and is sitting around the coffee table, on the floor. Everyone is sipping an adult beverage. Todd has rationed the beer, restricted hard booze to one double per evening, and flat out prohibited the use of Mind-Altering Drugs. Chocolate, although highly addictive, is exempt from such inhuman constraints. Depending on their personality traits, those present display moods that vacillate between euphoria and anxiousness.

"The ad in the *Tribune* has run. We have a contact phone. Let us hope that the wording scares away many a horny spinster." Some wit suggests that it is expected that their fearless leader perform "services beyond the call of duty" for the few hopeful female respondents.

"Here is the plan for the next steps," Todd offers, ignoring the catcalls these last remarks sired. "Two Draisine's have been parked on the spur track near Waldo. One for transporting the money, one as a diversion, as the shiny object. For the dimwits to follow." His by now well-known propensity to use misdirection, distractions and diversions is uniformly admired. The smarter ones among the group are silently hoping that the opposition, the Feds, are as incompetent, ignorant, and as dull as Todd's plans call for. Any idea that relies on the stupidity of the opposition is risky.

"How do we stop them from giving us forgeries, sequentially-numbered bills, or blank paper? Or movie-money bills?" an inquisitive mid inquires.

"We will force them to provide a currently incarcerated felon to verify the cash quantity and quality by random sampling. A retired forger. Found one in Oklahoma City. He's got two years to go on his sentence, nonviolent offender, well-behaved, hustling for an early release. I met the guy before his conviction. The Bureau of Prison is expected to support his parole. Half a suitcase will be waiting for him upon his release. Nice paycheck for one hour's worth of work."

The inquisitive mind is satisfied.

Todd is mighty proud of his solution for perhaps the most vexing problem of the heist. We must remember that this operation is more what Legal Scholars like to refer to as a blackmail op, rather than outright theft. No one really wants a Nuke—what one wants is the pile of cash that the previous owner is willing to shell out for its safe return. It is that exchange that requires a delicate, ingeniously intricate plan. Finding a way to return the Nuke during the trade is easy; getting away with the money is difficult. The first part of this challenge is overcome by keeping the location and the timing of the exchange a secret until the very last minute. Only the thieves will know where to set up a sniper, and then reveal the info that a sniper will be present, to keep everybody "Honest." For that reason alone, all this will take place, once again, in the middle of the night. The details of all this were kept a secret even from his team. Just in case one of the knowledgeable team members gets caught and then promptly subjected to waterboarding.

The few that have not ridden off into the sunset already have convened for the briefing in the media room of the rental home. Mike and Todd have wired their laptop to a substantial sized smart TV hanging on the wall. The arm wrestling with the setup took place a while back, and Bingo, up comes a Google map, with a satellite imagery overlay of the area between Bernalillo and Cerrillos. It shows a lot of desert, one major highway, and a bunch of county roads. There is nothing else out there. A bright green dot shows up next to the Bernalillo Railrunner shuttle parking; a second bright red dot appears at the Waldo ghost town.

Todd holds up his glass, swishing his Old-fashioned around to get at the smashed black cherries, he takes a sip, and then waves his hand for silence.

"Gentlemen, we are approaching the juicy part of this op. The part where they get their goody back, and we get our retirement funds. Or the seed capital for the next stupid idea." Chuckles abound.

Everyone, for the last few weeks, had been speculating on how the exchange will be pulled off. The tension is, therefore, thick as peanut butter. Todd's ego needs a reveal, something akin to the escape of the dove from a magician's hat. This is where a small audience is not an obstacle, and he will get to bask in his glory. Prematurely, for sure, since the object of his glory has dead Presidents printed on the front. And we aren't there yet. But getting very, very close.

Todd does not expose where the plan originated from – revealing that would put a dent in his glory-to-be-basked-in. The methodology, about to be explained to his team, (hold the last few bars from *Thus Spoke Zarathustra*), he actually pinched from a real crime that took place in Berlin in the nineties, a stunt orchestrated by a guy named Funke, better known as Dagobert. Days, weeks, researching successful blackmail operations led Todd to this morsel. Todd plans to take to his grave the fact that his brilliant plan is a copy, although with some improvements. Funke had terrorized Berlin's premier shops with bombings and occupied nearly the entire German police force for months.

"Ok, here's how this will go down. We will do two things right before the agreed-upon time of the exchange. We will stretch fishing line, five feet above the track across the track. The first one at Waldo, right where the ruins of the ovens are. The second one in the tunnel just south of the Interstate 550 turnoff in Bernalillo. That commuter parking lot at the Bernalillo Railrunner station is where this will go down. What's the fishing line for, you might want to ask? That will trigger a switch to stop the Draisine in case the radio link is interrupted. John, who will be the sniper, hidden a third of a mile away in the Placitas hills, will operate our little train. A second radio will be in the capable hands of Mike here, eagerly awaiting the arrival of the money in Waldo. You are getting the picture."

Now the questions start flying. "How is the Draisine propelled?" Electric, gasoline generator, battery backup. "How long does it take for the train to reach Waldo?" The track distance is just under 30 miles, so say 18 minutes. "When does the event take place?" We have a two-hour no-traffic-on-the track time window, starting at one a.m. "Will they send up helicopters with infrared imaging to chase the money?" Yep, they will. In time. "Enough time for us?" Enough time. "Won't every suitcase have a tracking transmitter?" Yes, and we will send the second Draisine with one suitcase—a horrible but essential sacrifice—screaming northbound towards Colorado. And the other twenty-four Samsonite's will be transferred to the Camper with the Faraday cage. "Where will we be heading?" Madrid, next door. A short drive, so our car does not leave a heat signature. Wait till the chopper is chasing the decoy. Then proceed to the airport parking where the fake commuter minivan awaits us.

Prepare to Execute the Deal

The interoffice memo, short, concise, and with a very much constrained distribution list, watermarked "Classified" on every page, is arriving at inboxes all over New Mexico. A few redacted copies already went to recipients in Washington DC. The full version reads as follows.

Subject Operation <u>HALO</u>. Update #6. Document release time is 11:28 Santa Fe time, 1728 UTC, 13:28 DC. Classified.

Status update: Operation <u>HALO</u> encompasses the retrieval of a stolen Pit in exchange for an undisclosed sum of cash, the pursuit of the perpetrators, and the reclaiming of the funds. A task force consisting of staff from relevant agencies has been formed and will operate under the alias

SUNSET. The particulars of the exchange as it stands to-day are:

The SUNSET team will assemble at the KSAF National Guard Hangars today at Five PM local time. A detailed briefing will start at Five Fifteen PM local time. The time and location of the exchange will not be known until later tonight. We were given a time for the next contact at six PM. Since the roadblocks failed to apprehend any of the participants of the raid, we assume that both men and our property had passed through the checkpoint locations before their deployment or bypassed the roadblocks on the night of the assault. Law enforcement is developing some leads, but does not have suspects at this time. By now, the Pit can be anywhere, but we expect that it is still in the Southwest. The objective of operation HALO, in sequence of priority, are:

1.　　Retrieval of the Pit
2.　　Capture of the perpetrators
3.　　Retrieval of the funds

Based on profiler analysis and best-practice prognosis, we have to be ready to, post-exchange, to intercept on public transport, surface vehicles, and aircraft. To keep their advantage, we expect to learn not until the last possible minute about the mechanics of the transfer. While unpredictable, we are suffering from a lack of information and the complexity of a multi-point objective list. Our opposition has but one purpose: getting away with the money. Up to this point, they have proven to be capable and competent. It is best to anticipate the continuation of such behavior.

The money has been packaged in twenty-five Samsonite suitcases. All the cases contain a hidden GPS tracking device. Their location can be polled via cellular networks. The cases are ready for the exchange on standard shipping pallets. We have been instructed to have readily accessible a forklift for loading. Logic suggests that a truck or a sizable aircraft will meet us. The Pit is unlikely to be at the exchange location at that time; more likely, we will learn where it can be picked up. Our opposition was eager to point out that they see this as a simple business transaction; they claim to have made "suitable" arrangements in case we deviate from the agreement we have reached. Violence, while undesirable, is not off the table, we have been informed.

End of report #6.

The Exchange

Soldiers are used to endless waits. Cops, not so much. Police officers are trained to take charge, right up until someone with more seniority shows up. Waiting cops pace, waiting soldiers squat. The briefing just after five, everyone was early, did not offer much new info. Now the painfully slow clock reveals that it is past seven; everybody is soaking wet by now, burdened by the massive and tight body armor. Trucks, police cars, and an ominous-looking dull black armored personnel carrier decorated with the words APD SWAT stenciled in white on the side are parked, the nose pointing towards the base exit. A State Police helicopter and a New Mexico National Guard Blackhawk, inspected and fueled, are sitting outside the hangar. The red "Remove before flight" streamers are still attached; the doors are open for ventilation, and the pilot's helmets are visible on their respective seats.

A brief burst from a siren that sounds like an old submarine ready to dive warns of an incoming announcement. A second later, all chatter silenced, a voice informs that "Ground vehicles will reposition to Bernalillo and assemble on the Lowe's parking lot, just off Interstate 550. Air assets will remain here." From the rear of the crowd, we hear "Gentlemen, start your engines," promptly cautioned by a less well-read but more mature voice that "Drive fifteen miles below the speed limit." Clouds of black smoke belches from exhausts, engines are revved up, and the convoy begins to sneak towards the gate. The drive to the staging area takes about an hour, the personnel carrier showing up last, hampered by a conservative speed limit to keep the run-flat tires, tires that can be shot at without going flat, from coming off the rims.

Not that the waiting is over. The soldiers know that, but the cops are blissfully ignorant of any applicable traditions. By twelve forty-five, the whole team moves again, this time to the Railrunner commuter parking. The last vehicle pulls in just as the first southbound freight train of the new day rumbles by. No more rail traffic is expected until five a.m. Eagle turns to his second in command and mumbles, "This is a stupid place to stage an exchange. There must be a surprise coming. What will the surprise be? A helicopter? They seem to like helicopters. If so, it will be a big mother. The two pallets are just a bit less than 900 pounds, but lots and lots of volume."

An officer from the U.S. Marshall service comes walking up. He was not briefed on what is going on here, he was simply told to bring a convict from the FCI El Reno prison in Oklahoma City for unspecified reasons. He is not amused by the silent treatment and his self-introduction reflects that. He opens with "Hi. I have a convict from the El Reno facility back in the car. Guy by the name of Wilson, Mitchell. He is supposed to perform some magic that only he can perform."

"Bring him over" is all he is privileged to hear. He does a one-eighty on his heels and storms off, returning with a mid-thirty-year-old, sort of academic-looking man in an orange jumpsuit and leg irons. No handcuffs. Matt, having shed his business uniform in exchange for a blue windbreaker steps up and says "I'll take it from here. Take his restraints off. Have you seen how much Law Enforcement is hanging around here? Where is he going to go and how far do you think he will get?" Standard protocol, Matt is told. The restraints come off anyway. As Matt leads his prisoner over to the pallets, he introduces himself. "I realize that you do have the time, and possibly the inclination for this task. We appreciate your cooperation and we hope that this is no great inconvenience for you." Had he said that to a paid consultant this would have sounded polite and friendly. Saying the same words to a convict makes it sound like an insult covered in inch-thick sarcasm. He continues with "I see no need to reiterate the arrangement between you and the parole board. You are here to check some currency samples. You will inspect two suitcases full of US currency. You pick the cases. After you are done, we will wait for a phone call. You will answer the caller's questions. This whole op is the end of a blackmail exchange. The caller represents the Crooks. If you screw them, they will come and kill you. If you screw us, we will slap another five years of solitary onto you sentence. If all goes well, whatever god you pray to will look kindly upon your parole request. Questions?"

Mister Wilson goes to work.

Eagle does not have to wait long. A voice, half-covered by a screech, ends with "tdrrrrk vekkl coming." Eagle rips the radio from the nearest sweaty figure and says, "Inaudible. Repeat." By now, a Draisine approaching from the north comes into view, slows to a halt right in front of the big truck that brought in the forklift and the money. A repeat is no longer required. Hidden rifles point towards the door of the bright yellow front, the crew cab, the low loading deck behind. No one emerges. The cell phone rings.

He picks up. "Is Mitchell there?" He is indeed. "Has he done his job?" He has. "Put him on." The phone changes hands. Eagle, Matt and a bunch of uniforms remain within earshot. All that can be heard is one side of the conversation. Al lot of Yes's and No's, some I Guess's. And a You are welcome. The phone goes back to Matt. "Satisfied? Are we good?" Satisfied.

Eagle grabs the cell from Matt and waits. "Ready?" a voice says.

"Whenever you are," Eagle responds. "Load the pallets now" he hears. He is quickly informed that after a count of ten, the exchange is off, unless the forklift starts moving pallets, pronto. Ahh, so they are watching us. A muffled conversation ensues among the good guys. Eye contact is out of the question, it being pitch black outside. No one is foolish enough to step into any light. Eagle ends the stalemate by saying, "Remember: Priority One." Seconds later the forklift is inching towards the open end of the truck. "We want to see the Pit case, with the cover open, under the light, before we load the second pallet." The case is, of course, not here.

A text message, no text, but two picture attachments arrives. The first is a picture, adequately lit and framed, of the open Pit case, the stenciled serial number clearly readable. The second picture is a close-up of a small piece of paper; the top lines smeared over a name and an address with a wide black sharpie. Right below is a five-digit number. A luggage tag? Receipt from a pawn shop? No way to know from whom. The voice on the cell asks, "Got the pictures?" Yes, we got it. "When the last pallets are loaded, we will depart. Stay clear of the track. Once it, I mean the train, is moving, I will tell you where to pick up your device. If you interfere, follow or chase us, we will remote detonate the case. Most of the building will go with it. Here's a hint: it's a hotel. Full of people."

Eagle shakes his head. Outmaneuvered again. The bomb is probably a bluff. Eagle holds down the mute button and he screams "Bomb Tech. Here. Now." He cannot take the risk that it is NOT a bluff. Into the dark one barely hears Eagle say, to no one in particular, "Once that guy is out of prison, I want his résumé on my desk." The last pallet is on the Draisine by now. Slowly it starts moving back where it came from. Todd says, "The Hyatt. Downtown Albuquerque. Ask the bellboy. Bye-bye."

Once out of sight, one can hear the generator screaming, the Draisine picking up speed, and the sounds from the track gradually dissipating. Eagle knows he is screwed. Over his shoulder he says to Matt "Tell your boys to see if they can get a location or better yet a track. And get the Blackhawk in the air."

The Cash

John watches in fascination from his lair, a bit up and away from the Commuter Parking Lot and the train tracks. The show reminds him of a thriller video with no audio and no subtitles, but with a solid knowledge of the plot. It is not difficult to piece together what is going on down there. The moment the Draisine speeds off into the dark, he picks up his gear, climbs into his car and heads up and away, fearing a possible search party. As a sniper with solid training, he had searched for the best elevated view; obviously it would not be difficult for the law to arrive at the same conclusion.

Placitas can supposedly only be reached via a dead-end street, so they might simply be waiting for him at the bottom of the incline where the I25 on-ramp is situated. Scouting missions in preparation for this part of the show, however, did demonstrate that a dirt road, for off-road vehicles only, that keeps going towards the Sandia Ski basin, offers a safe way out. The road's condition assures a miserable ride. Potholes, smallish boulders, and branches need to be navigated. No street lights, no guard rails. No traffic. No houses. No dogs. No signs of a human presence. New Mexico at its finest.

Meanwhile, Todd and the remnants of his army are pacing the gravel around their camper at the Waldo rail spur. Mike just returned from a climb down from a bunch of tall rocks, tall enough to offer minimal one-bar cell reception. "John called from half-way up Sandia Peak. The stuff is on its way. Departure time was 22 minutes after the hour; ETA here is now 40 after the hour."

The wait is unbearable. Checking the time every three minutes does not help. But still, it is something to do. The back of the camper is open and empty. Mike has the most sensitive ears, and he is the first who detects the faint engine noises of the generator. Todd is holding one of the remotes, ready to bring the oncoming Draisine to a halt right behind the second, identical unit waiting on the track. Todd is wearing night vision goggles. As the platform with the suitcases comes into focus, he lets out some uncharacteristic expletives, and he would have made Samuel L. Jackson proud, as he sees one of the straps, that is supposed to hold all the cases in place, flapping in the light breeze.

"Let's get cracking. We only have a few minutes. Count the cases during the transfer. Put one case in the back of the other, the wild-goose-chase Draisine." A voice from the dark in front of the assembled group running back and forth, two cases at a time, calls out, "One case is now on the beast. Let it run." Todd grabs the second remote, punches a few buttons, and watches a yellow blur disappear in the darkness. "Go on, track that, my friends." Somewhere short of Lamy, the cell signal will come online again, and the helicopter will surely be right behind.

"Do we have a count?" Yes, one case just departed, by now hopefully the subject of a wild goose chase. Twenty-three are in the camper, Todd hears. So, one fell off when the belt came loose, somewhere between the parking lot and Waldo. No one is going to look for it, at least not one of us, Todd thinks. The cargo door clicks as it closes, and with broad grins on their faces, the team quietly sneaks through sleeping Cerrillos and Madrid towards Albuquerque Sunport.

Erin and the Money

A text message from the Lab, addressing me formally as Mister Harry S. Anderson, alerts me that they wish to fly with me this morning. The message contains a phone number, not the one from which the message originated. Call before nine am, it says. Call from the airport and be ready to depart for two and one-half hours—one passenger sitting in the right rear, doors off. Ok, got it. Seven is not the right time to call the FBI. I don't like talking on the phone while the called individual is munching donuts. Correction: this is the FBI, not the cops, so they would be munching Eggs Benedict, instead.

Gradually I am beginning to piece together what is—or better was—going on here. While the interview by the fellow Matt had sent over was quite lengthy, it did not provide any new significant insights on my part. His purpose was to gather facts, not leak information. For a cop, the interviewer was restrained, almost shy. Maybe he recently graduated from Quantico? He took notes on a yellow legal type pad, with very delicate handwriting; he also wrote down the questions, not just my response.

I am about to leave when I get a second text message saying "No need to call unless you can't help us. Let's meet at the airport at nine-thirty. Bring a photographer with a DSLR for the front left seat." Now where in the hell am I supposed to find a photographer between seven-thirty and nine thirty? In the morning?

I have a bright idea. I call Erin. She picks up on the third ring. She knows about Ian from the newscast, and when she asks me how I am doing, she means how do I handle the loss of my friend. I tell her that we might have time to talk about it later, but right now, I need to know three things: Does she own a digital camera—not an iPhone—but a Cannon or a Nikon or similar device? She does. Next: Is she available today to join me and take pictures? She is. And at last: Does she want some more flight time in the Long Ranger? Man, she says, does she ever. She will meet me at the airport. Via Uber, her car is in the shop. Can I drop her off at home afterwards? I can.

By now I am at the hangar, observing the tug pull out the Ranger. The fuel truck is right behind. When looking around on the ramp, I am surprised to find that the Huey is gone. As my eyes sweep the National Guard Hangars, I discover that the Crook's Huey is sitting on their ramp, with four guys in white coveralls crawling around inside and out. It is impossible to tell what they are doing. Collecting evidence, I suppose. All other guard aircraft are either in the closed hangar or are out flying.

Before I can make the call, while I am gathering my helmet, two spare helmets for the passenger, and paperwork odds and ends, the open door on my office darkens as a State Trooper blocks the outside view. Nobody I have ever met before. Tight uniform shirt, sharp creases on shirt and pants, black shoes honed to a glossy shine. He is a bit older with a bunch of stripes that must define his seniority but mean nothing to me. He must have lived in the South somewhere; his accent reminds me of Jim Nabors and I am anticipating that he'll introduce himself as Beauregard. After a brief intro without mentioning his name for now, he shares the objective of today's flight.

"Early in the investigation, we established that the raid at the Lab was well-planned, concocted, and executed. Some of the vehicles used in the raid, many later abandoned, have been found nearby. We also found that at least one vehicle from the raid was located where another car was parked for a few days before the raid. A local cop ticketed it for obstructing traffic and a broken taillight. This guy actually ticketed a parked car for a broken taillight. Now we want to look around for other vehicles that might have played a role before, during, or after the raid. Whatever was stolen from Los Alamos is now back where it belongs, so the worst stress is over. Broken Arrow has been canceled, HALO is still on. The plan is to start this flight in Bernalillo and follow the Amtrak line as far as Raton. Is your photographer here?" Not yet. But she is on the way.

I hear a car horn. An unwashed Honda Civic, minor dents only, is sitting in front of the gate. I walk out and over to press the button; the gate opens. Erin climbs out, grabs her backpack, approaches. A firm handshake? Is that a fitting welcome for a current lover? She realizes that there is no reason to let the fuzz know that we are friends. I so love smart, perceptive people.

Jack has removed all the doors, front and rear, and tied them down in the back behind Erin's seat. There to be re-installed, just in case this takes longer, and the forecast turns out to be correct, threatening us with a cold front, winds expected at 35 knots from the north. Erin belts herself in; I check that the helmet fits, and I plug it in for her. She looks breathtaking. I walk around to the back, and I find the Trooper has done a similarly fine job; this is not his first rodeo either.

The battery comes on. The tanks are full. I do an intercom check; all three of us fiddle with the various ways to adjust the volume. "Set it louder than what is comfortable now, and make a final adjustment once the engine is running," I advise. "And make sure that the noise canceling is on. It'll be noisy with the doors off."

No traffic is in the air, an Embraer from American is taxiing in. We are cleared southbound. Scrutinizing the highway shoulders makes no sense, so I center the skids on the single railroad track heading south. One more volume check, then I grab Erin's idle hand and silently put it on the cyclic, while her left hand finds the collective. She looks like the personification of self-confidence. The camera is on the floor between her feet. I glance at the instruments. Altitude, heading, and torque get a B+. I am torn between pride—after all, it was me who taught her to fly this thing, and admiration for how much of a natural she is.

The flight to the parking lot is fast and short. All that is left on the platform from last night is some yellow Police "No Access" tape, whose loose ends flap vigorously in the wind. The forecast was right. She does a spacious one-eighty, slows down to forty knots, and descends to one hundred feet above the tracks. Jake, the cop, I now remember his name again, seems happy but asks for a move a bit to the left, since he is trying to check things on the ground out of the open door-frame on the right side. Erin is busy flying, I am busy doing nothing, and Jake is concentrating, looking for cars that don't belong, for tire tracks in the sparse dried grass—anything out of the ordinary.

At some point, the track veers to the right and passes through a short tunnel underneath the Interstate. As we cross over the freeway, I hear Jake say, "Stop here and circle back" in a low, but alert, tone of voice. Stop? No wonder they wanted a helicopter. Then I see it: a few green pieces of paper are being tossed around in the air. Money? We circle; more green papers. He wants me to land. Erin and I both look for a decent spot to land. I point to a flat place next to the freeway and the tracks, right where the train exits the tunnel.

For a second or two, I turn the intercom to "Pax Isolate," so that Jake can't hear us, and say "Want me to take it?" and I get an amused "No thanks. Piece of cake. Go back to sleep," in return. The intercom goes back to "All." I get to admire yet another fine piece of flying as Erin does a low approach over a fence—a touch too low for my comfort as the tail rotor barely clears the fence that keeps deer off the Interstate. She touches down. The collective is lowered, the rotor winds down to idle. Jake says, "Let me out, I wanna walk over to the underpass." I signal to Erin to stay put, and I get out at the same time as Jake. Chopper pilots are always nervous about passengers walking into the spinning tail rotor. By the time I am out of my seat, Jake is already down an embankment heading for the tunnel entrance. "Right behind you," I yell over the engine noise.

It's money, alright. Not much of it, but enough to justify a slow walk on the center of the track. And there it is: laying next to the track is a busted hard-shell Samsonite, a fist-sized hole in the side, dollar bills pulling out in the draft, one or two at the time. I turn to Jake and propose that we drag the suitcase back up the incline and put it in the cargo bay. No reason to lose more of Uncle Sam's property. The damn thing is heavier and more cumbersome than either of us are prepared for, but after some cursing, slipping and dragging, we make it, and the case ends up in the cargo bay. Right before I close and latch that door, I see that a few wires are protruding through the cases lining out of the hole.

"Let's go back and check what else is down there. Also, let's collect the loose bills, if any." My path to the tunnel leads past Erin, both her hands at the controls, looking at me. I catch up with Jake, and we start picking up twenties and fifties. While bent down we try to find out how and why that suitcase got there. As we get to the end of the tunnel on the far side, I hear the aircraft engine pick up speed. I curse and dash back towards the tunnel entrance, emerging at the exact moment the downdraft from the blades blows all manner of dust in my face. I rub my eyes so I can see again and feel a chill when I see the tail boom of my helicopter, featuring Erin and a pile of money, clear the fence outbound and disappear over the freeway. Southbound.

Sunport to Juarez

The mere fact that no one seemed interested in the camper, the day after the raid, provided clear evidence that the Faraday cage, as far as radio signals were concerned, was leakproof. An alternative explanation would be that the suitcases contained no tracking device; no one actually believed that such a pile of money would be so casually abandoned. It had not taken long to find and remove the tracking chips buried in the cases liner. It had taken the border patrol months, if not years, to collect all those precisely bundled bills. When drugs cross the border from Mexico, shortly before or shortly thereafter, the cash follows south across the same border. The money is easier to find than the drugs: every street dealer in the States who is observed doing business can lead to the next level of management. As financial responsibility rises, so does the size of the stash. At some point in the organizational pyramid, like in any other business venture, some grizzled veteran of the drug trade has P&L responsibility. That's the guy the border patrol wants to catch. So, somehow, somewhere, putting a tracker into a bundle of money seems to lead to seizures. No way, Mike claims, will twenty-five million US dollars be left unprotected. Hence the Faraday cage. The trailer, with the identical advertising on the back as the van, was subjected to the same treatment as the rear of the camper.

At the Sunport, parked in the shuttle bus parking lot, the nicely decorated van sits, a little dustier than it was when dropped off, with a trailer still attached. John gets out of the RV, fires up the van, and follows the RV out of the parking lot. One of the researchers had previously done a decent job on two scouting missions to find a spot for the transfer of both men and suitcases, where such activity would not garner attention, nor leave behind evidence, such as a video recording. Twentieth-and-some-century America seems to have a video camera hanging from every power pole, every streetlight. Even along the interstate, there are masts sprouting video surveillance installations every couple of miles. Ultimately a compromise decision was reached. Along East Central Avenue, a whole slew of failed Camper dealers left behind open spaces, now cluttered with empty freight containers scattered in a most disgusting disorderly fashion all over their lots. No visible cameras, no security staff, no gate, nada. Todd had only seen pictures when he approved the choice of the location that ended up on a humble shortlist. He is now as pleased with the real thing as he was with the photos.

As the camper pulls into the space, he directs the vehicles into an area that is so far back that he asks, "Are we still in New Mexico?" He chooses a spot where the camper and the van can be backed-in close to the wall at the rear of the lot. The camper's open rear door, and the trailer's rear door end up, after some jostling back and forth, merely a foot and a half apart. Mike climbs into the trailer and starts pulling out covers, all the same size, but different fabric colors. Protection for the twenty-eight inch Samsonite's.

"Everybody step inside, please grab a suitcase, pull the cover over it and stack them in the trailer." This is fun. Everybody is in a great mood. Mike decides to pull Todd's leg by stating that "I did not realize to what extent a sense of fashion was a job requirement."

Todd smiles a little and says, "Just in case we get pulled over, and the fuzz wants to peek into the trailer. Our pursuers chose the suitcases; they know what they look like. An APB describing them must be out by now." The whole operation is over and done within just under half an hour. Three covers are unused: one that was ordered as a spare, one intended for the lost case, and one for the sacrifice they made in honor of the goose chase to Raton. John pulls the van forward; everybody gets out, and someone is about to close the door of the trailer, leaving the unused covers behind in the RV, when Todd intervenes. "Don't leave the covers behind, you twerp, the idea was to change the look into something unknown. Jesus, why am I cursed with amateurs." He's not really serious. The RV is wiped down for fingerprints, the empties are collected, and the RV is abandoned.

Mike, now driving, heads down Central to the interstate, climbs the ramp and merges onto the southbound lane. "Smoke 'em if you have 'em," someone suggests. No one has em – health advice and cancer has turned smoking into an ancient habit. "It will take about four hours to get to the border. Relax. If we have to explain ourselves, we are going to Juarez and then on to Chihuahua. We are engineers heading south to train Mexicans, working at our factory."

Project Halo

S pending time at home, for those times when your tools and your toys have been stolen, can be leisurely and rewarding. It can also be a time filled with frustration and self-chastisement, where one's mood oscillates between anger and sadness. It is one full day after the flight with Jake and Erin. Nobody refers to it as The Fire anymore. I spent the better part of the morning hustling the insurance company. Customer service for an insurance company must mean a toll-free call and hold music. I recognize Rodrigo's "Concierto de Aranjuez" performed by Pepe Romero.

After listening to the triage lecture, I press many a button that led straight back to the main menu and having said "Agent" a few fruitless times I give up. Maybe the Lab can help—they carry blanket insurance for flights conducted on their behalf.

Having temporarily abandoned the pursuit of compensation for my helicopter, I turn my attention to an equally pressing matter.

Erin. My brilliant idea to leave her sitting at the controls at idle makes me at least partly culpable, of course. It had been me who created the actual opportunity. That said: Exactly when did she decide to haul ass with a million dollars? When she saw the fifties float in front of the bubble? Or was I the chump in a setup? Did she show up at the EAA meeting at the Double Eagle Airport, fluttering her lashes, intent on screwing me—pun intended? Or anywhere in between? If it was a setup, when and how did she perceive the opportunity? None of these alternatives make spontaneous sense to me. And most pressing of all, was her affection real or fake?

The cell phone vibrates, I managed to grab it just as it's about to fall off the desk.

It's Matt. Eagle has been recalled to Washington for meetings. A promotion perhaps? More likely castration. With a rusty Machete. Project HALO, the pursuit of the Crooks, is now a standard robbery slash blackmail investigation. Matt, with poorly concealed pride in his voice, announces that he's in charge now. A paper pusher? They picked a paper pusher? Although he was handed a stinking mess, he seems happy.

"Here is a status update: HALO has been ruled a fully grown clusterfuck, Madam Secretary's words, not mine. What she meant is that the loss of twenty-four million dollars in cash, we retrieved the one case in Raton, and the near loss of a multi-million-dollar Pit can under no circumstances be declared a success. And the perpetrators are sipping cocktails on a beach somewhere by now. To top things off, the political appointees in DC have backdated HALO to have started when we first stumbled on the game cameras. Now that the first half of the game, the half we soundly lost, is over, with twenty-twenty hindsight, we are reminded what glaringly obvious warnings we missed. Out of fear of over alerting those we suspected to be involved in who-knows-what we failed to put them under physical surveillance. Instead we used our competitors at the NSA—an agency not authorized to operate in the fifty states—to collect SIGINT."

I interject with "I know what Signal Intelligence is." I don't reveal that there is sufficient evidence that ol Matt here had the NSA listening in on MY phone calls as well.

Matt continues "We kept pursuing burner phones and pre-paid debit cards, tossed after the first traceable use. Etcetera. And, I truly hate to say this, we did not pay enough attention to your words of warning. Make you feel good?"

Angry, I belt out, "Getting my fucking helicopter back would make me feel good." Getting Ian back would help as well. And once I figured out what Erin's role in this was, *maybe* getting Erin back would help? Perhaps you could offer some support related to my insurance claim?

He continues with what he euphemistically refers to as a request for help. I stop him right there and point out that so far, this whole exercise has been an unmitigated disaster for me. So better make it enjoyable. This time. I continue, "You always call me when you want to force me into deciding on the spot, without much time for me to ponder the big picture. If it is a harmless request, you send a text message I noticed. Alas, by all means, proceed."

Matt has developed an uncanny ability to ignore my sarcasm, and he goes on with "You know, experience shows that in every major crime with lots of participants, someone somehow somewhere fucks up. Well, this

277

morning, someone complied with this theory and used a debit card, one that had been used before at a hotel in Santa Fe, to prepay room reservations in Divisadero in Mexico. The name of one of the guests is Morales. Probably a fake, matching his driver's license. Two rooms. No connecting door. Check-in is tomorrow; guest arriving by train." Matt must have sensed me holding up my hand. "Where the hell is Divisadero, and what train goes there?"

The train, I learn, is called Ferrocarril Barrancas del Cobre, more casually abbreviated to El Chepe, and runs between Chihuahua and Los Mochis in Mexico. That train stops at Divisadero. Nothing there except a hotel or two and one hell of a view of Copper Canyon, the Grand Canyon of Mexico. The nearest town is Creel. Both the resort and Creel have airports with miserably short runways. The biggest plane into either runway was, up to now, a DeHavilland Twin Otter.

"So, we are planning to be in place to meet whoever shows up. Meet them with a hostage rescue team. The Mexican Marines, the only law enforcement we trust to not be compromised, will send someone, to make whatever goes down tomorrow legal. We would like for you to join us for this: you are the only one who has seen some or many of the individuals we are looking for while they were in Santa Fe."

I pause. If it were not for the need to seek revenge for Ian, I would flatly refuse. Matt misinterprets the pause as a sign of compliance. He asks, "What size are you? Height, weight, waist?" Measuring me for the casket? No, it turns out that protocol requires a body armor for all invitees. We haggle about reimbursement. I win. I assure him I'll be there early tomorrow, for a flight to Creel. A long flight in uncomfortable seats, I am promised.

The flight took forever. First, we left Santa Fe in a Cessna Citation with civilian markings and headed to Chihuahua. That took one and one-half hour, in great comfort.

We were four of us, civilian clothing—nothing to offend the Mexican's eternal sensitivity about their sovereignty. In Chihuahua, we picked up four guys from the Marines. They looked in shape, dressed in green jumpsuits, covered with body armor, and a vest to store a warrior's junk in an enormous number of pockets. One carried a twelve-gauge shotgun. The transfer to an aging Twin Otter dressed up as a plane for parachute operations preceded the introductions. Their team leader, same physiognomy as a younger Pancho Villa, did not say much, the rest of his team said nothing. All seats had been removed to accommodate the jumpers, so we sat on the floor for forty-five minutes. The promised lack of comfort kicked in about ten minutes into the flight. That flight took us directly to Divisadero. On the map, the airport is marked Pista Barrancas del Cobre.

I fell asleep, waking up when I heard the flaps come down and the pitch of the props change as we turned onto a long final. There are power lines stretched right at the approach end. Someone had the decency to put an orange ball in the center. The short final is, therefore, longer than anyone wished for, at the same time shrinking the runway length left after touchdown short enough to dispense vast amounts of hormones into one's bloodstream. I know that the runway ends at the cliff. An adverse outcome would be to be too fast to stop, but not fast enough to open the throttle and fly a missed approach. With about two hundred feet to spare, we taxied over to park under the trees. A well-developed sense of mistrust lead to the decision to arrive unannounced. This is cartel country after all.

Matt points out that there will be, as he put it ". . . no one to meet us. We led them to expect that we will be on the terrain ourselves."

The hotel must not have heard us arrive so no one comes to pick us up; we march in a single file from the airport to the hotel, a nice walk through an anorexic pine forest. We are early, but not by much. Pancho steps ahead to talk with the manager who generously offers a small meeting room for us to gather and deposit our stuff. Resorts around these parts show great respect and courtesy to the Federales and the Marines. We Americans decide to keep our mouths shut and play dumb. When asked, the manager walks us over to the room set aside for Mister Morales, next to one connecting room for an unnamed and gender-undefined visitor. Clearly no one read the booking request with the expected diligence: the reservation called for non-connecting rooms. We have an hour to check out the hotel before El Chepe is expected from Chihuahua. The hotel turns out to be a charming, an older place built right on top of the cliff with balconies protruding out over the void, perfect for introducing guests to acrophobia.

Matt and Pancho position most of the Marines at the exits, leaving the main entry into the lobby seemingly unguarded. Matt changes into a loose windbreaker hanging over his belt. He takes a seat in the hall, right behind the entrance. The idea is to approach Mister Morales while he is checking in, since the corridors leading to the rooms are narrow and sparingly lit and have been deemed useless for an initial approach. The Marines will stay out of sight unless their presence is requested. In a few minutes, I will be joining Matt to identify anyone I recognize. And we will now wait.

The Shoot Out

Just about half an hour before we expect Morales to emerge from the train, we hear the horn announcing another train's arrival. Must be one of the local commuter trains. I step into our room to put on my body armor and slip into a windbreaker for cover. None of us who came from the States is armed; this resulted from the arrangement negotiated between Washington and Mexico City. I am at ease with this, since I had the privilege of taking a good look at the passengers that joined us in the Twin Otter. These are tough hombres, a team comfortable with each other, well equipped, and at ease.

I step out into the hallway and proceed to the lobby to join Matt. I casually mention to Matt that "I have never been protected with that much firepower." There is bright sunshine outside. However, the lobby, is, for someone

281

stepping in from outside, pretty dark. Matt is sitting on a sofa, and I am standing next to him, leaning against the wall. We still have nearly one hour to go.

Two men walk into the lobby, followed at some distance by a bellboy. It's Mike and John.

They took the train from Los Mochis; they came in just now; while we were looking in the wrong direction. They must initially have flown to Los Mochis. It's frustrating to realize that, one more time, we screwed up. We? I feel a need to blame Matt – I am here as a witness. Only as a witness.

They walk right past us, protected from discovery by the dark lobby and by their sunglasses, and they lean up against the check-in counter. Based on what Pancho must have told the manager, no one from the hotel is discernible.

Mike hits the bell on the counter, twice, showing poor manners.

I put my hand on Matt's arm as he gets up as well. I suppose that my posture tells him everything he needs to know.

And now, time seems to have come to a standstill. Actually, it's all over in just a few seconds.

John takes off his sunglasses, blinks once, and turns around to check out the lobby. He sees me. His jaw drops, he is confused, a look of surprise worthy of an Oscar. "I watched you shoot the bastard," he says. Mike now turns around as well, just as John reaches into the small of his back. What emerges in John's right hand is a Smith and Wesson Saturday night special. A short-barreled revolver that looks like a 38, lots of punch but useless at distances over five feet. Just as he brings it up towards me, a Marine steps out from behind a bookshelf with his automatic shotgun pointing in the general direction of John. Not fast enough, for as the barrel of the gun slowly, ever so slowly it seems, rises, and John manages to get one round off, hitting the Marine in the center of the chest. A lucky shot. On his way backwards and down, the Marine lets the weapon drop to the floor. I bend down and grab the gun, just as John fires two more rounds, this time in my direction, but misses by two feet. I fire the shotgun once, and the recoil nearly sets me on my ass. I see what must be buckshot hit the target mid-chest. John is flung back against the counter. I quickly turn the gun towards Mike, who is tugging like crazy behind his back to release a weapon from a holster. I am barely on stable footing again when my first shot in his direction takes the muscle of his right thigh down to the bone, and the second shot hits the center of the chest. My third shot removes the top of his skull.

I turn towards John, who is sitting upright, on the floor, with his back against the counter. With an ashen face he looks down at the puddle of blood he is sitting in. His head tilts to the side as he passes out. There is tissue and blood everywhere. From the hotel: not a soul in sight.

I set down the shotgun and walk over to the Marine. He is conscious but in pain. The close range shot probably broke a couple of ribs when the bullet slammed into his body armor. I look up at Matt. He seems to be busy absorbing the events of the last few seconds. Matt doesn't have a scratch. Neither do I. I hear myself say, "You didn't think I had it in me, did you?" in the direction of the deceased beneficiaries of my rage.

Harry's Harvest

Matt's invitation arrives as a text message for a meeting to do some mopping up and to decide who is at fault. I'll be delighted to attend. On occasion, I enjoy watching the spewing of blame for a disaster among the innocent and the heaping of praise upon the guilty.

As to dress code: anything north of semi-casual will be considered gross, he says.

Very few show up. Jane, my instructor in the fine craft of espionage, walks over to say hi. Matt's second in command, the name no longer available to me, is silently sipping a diet coke. I get introduced to Jason, he who found the game camera. Al I had first met at one of the initial meetings. A few of the invisible back-office type, re-searchers, analysts, eavesdroppers have been invited here to massage their egos. After all, they can now claim to have participated in a counterterrorism campaign, and that will look good on their CV. Some anecdotes from this op, most within walking distance of the truth, are shared.

Everybody ends up sitting around the conference table. Matt cracks a few lame warm-up jokes. He reads from a prepared script, a letter of resignation by Whom We Called Eagle. So, he observes quietly, "So, they reached fairly high for a sacrificial lamb, this time." Eagle stayed true to form and style, omitting the usual '. . .Written in sorrow, not in anger. . .' bullshit. More like '. . .the time has come for a new generation. . . .' I had grown to like him, to admire his resilience, his instincts on how he picks his team members. Another fine public servant bites the dust, sacrificed on the altar of Public Relations. I decide then and there to track him down and offer to share a glass of fine wine.

This meeting will be brief, Matt insists. Reports need to be written. First drafts or outlines are due tomorrow by nine-hundred hours. Assignments as per memo. Then come the endless thank-yous covering the full Monty, from the Santa Fe Sheriff to the US Marshals Service to the State Troopers.

I am introduced at the end and I earn a round of polite if somewhat unenthusiastic applause. And then, right then and there, Matt is pleased to announce that all charges against me have been dropped.

"Dropped all charges? Are you fucking kidding me? What charges? I saved your fucking ass! You were a half-second away from taking a .357 slug in your chest. And let me tell you: that cardboard body armor you dispensed to us will not stop that." As I kick open the door on the way out without touching the door handle, I hear glass break.

I hear him yell, "Excessive force." Followed by "There is more!"

I leave long, black, smoking tire marks, I am so pissed off.

At the speed I am going it does not take long to get home. Zorro is trying to interpret my shitty mood; he quickly realizes that the blame has already been firmly attached to someone else.

At some point I begin to realize that I must have missed one or more possible explanation for the utterance that sent me into outer space. Charges? By whom, under whose jurisdiction? I must remember that the prisons are full with people 'who done nuttin wrong'.

And what did he mean when he yelled after me that "…there is more?"

A few hours later, I have since simmered down quite a bit, I hear a car door slammed shut.

Matt cannot find the doorbell behind the screen and raps politely at the window. My spontaneous first words are "You again." He is wearing the dark suit. His shiny polished black shoes now are covered in a light layer of dust from my parking lot – and I hope that this pisses him off royally.

"Can I come in?"

I hesitate and then with a gallant bow, and low and slow wave of the hand I solicit his admittance. As he walks by, I see that he gently shakes his head in disgust. I hear myself say "Be seated." He's here and he's not enjoying himself. This will be interesting.

Matt smiles, admittedly an astonishing display of a talent I had not previously observed in him, and he starts with "Some clarification might be in order: what I meant to say is that the Mexicans ruled the double homicide at Divisadero to be a justified use of force. You were never formally charged with anything other than one missing little bottle of scotch out of the minibar."

My response is a fairly loud. "Then why did you not say so in the first place?'

"I was building up the tension, for the drama, for what I was planning to say next. I never had a chance to do that, since you stormed out of the building. You broke the glass of the window in the door. We will deduct that from what we owe you." I have no idea what he's talking about; I figured I must have busted the glass, but my last bill was for the short one-way trip to where Erin left us standing in the blowing tumbleweed and that bill was settled a day or so ago.

Whatever comes next must be more enjoyable than admitting to literary shortcomings. He pulls out a small card with his notes. We are getting formal, are we?

"I suppose you never heard of the Atomic Weapons Rewards Act of 1955, Public Law 84-165, that authorizes financial transactions for information pertaining to the unlawful acquisition, importation, or manufacture of special nuclear material into the continental United States. The United States federal statute specifies financial reward payments of fifty thousand dollars be approved by the United States President with an inclusion not to exceed five hundred thousand dollars." I can confirm that I have not heard of that statute.

"Good to hear. Then it is with great pleasure that I can, on behalf of the Department of Energy and The Los Alamos National Laboratory, inform you that you have been awarded the stately sum of four hundred thousand dollars, minus the fifty bucks for the door, under that statute. It was your powers of observation, your efforts to inform us of events taking place that seem out of the ordinary and your report and later cooperation with us, that has led to the benign conclusion of this episode. Congratulations."

Erin Sends A Message

I spend an enormous amount of time, energy, and money dealing with the loss of the Long Ranger. It is hard to believe that something this big and colorful can simply disappear, especially since an aircraft is assembled from thousands of parts with carefully tracked serial numbers and, therefore, if taken apart in a chop-shop, is of little commercial value. If it is still in one piece, airworthy and being flown, it is even more useless, given the amount of publicity and media coverage the whole event received. Somebody somewhere will see it. Just wait.

I am getting some unenthusiastic help from LANL, and with some pushing and shoving comes a list of referrals about whom to talk to. All I can do is wander from one office to another, making friendly noises, flirt with the foxes when it's called for or drop off pralines on the desks of the chubbier secretaries who are defending the inner sanctum office doors. All chubby secretaries savor chocolate; some will sell their first-borne for truffles.

I have very little leverage; the secrecy agreement I signed a while back has provided me with an escape hatch because, when pursued by the press, I can say that a non-disclosure agreement binds me. At the same time, having to keep my mouth shut deprives me of the ability to hint at leaks to the press as a means of enticing support from an uncooperative administration.

My single biggest arm-wrestling contest is with the insurance company (with the leasing company mere inches behind). As one would expect, they are facing an unusual claim: most claims are for damages or destruction of an aircraft—theft is not unheard of, but rare. The insurance is asking for a scary multitude of documents in triplicate on embossed government letterhead that, whoever is supposed to supply the prose, is reluctant to provide. The first draft from the Santa Fe Sheriff's Office was a true masterpiece in saying essentially nothing on three pages. After much whining, I got a letter from Eagle's ex-assistant, also saying virtually nothing either, however, on one single page.

I am sitting at home, rather than at the airport since I have nothing to fly. The State Police had made a generous offer to supply enough manpower to deal with my unwarranted, unwelcome celebrity status. I took them up on this offer. I had some luck getting the cops to chase away the paparazzi from my airport presence, while I spend my days on the phone and dealing with a flurry of emails.

No sign nor sound from Erin. When I am awake and busy with work, I speculate about the likely benign, perhaps even positive explanation of what happened. At night, I do not do much sleeping these days, I sweat and toss and have much darker visions on what went down. Questions plague me: Did she seek me out from day one back in Albuquerque and set me up, or did she recognize at some point an opening and an opportunity way too sweet to pass up? The most relevant question, of course, is: Did she bend my beloved Long Ranger? It had been me after all, prompted by lousy judgment and lust, who had offered free stick time. I am willing to admit that it would have taken only mild additional enticement for me to provide more flight instruction, flights that I can neither afford or that I am formally qualified for. In retrospect, I recognize that I failed to appreciate the talent that she had for the job, but flying was a skill she was really adept at picking up—skilled enough to get away from me.

As the sun starts to set and shines on the dust on my desk, I decide to call it a day. Zorro has dragged his empty bowl from the kitchen as a reminder that right now, some food would be helpful. This represents the subtle approach—he is totally capable of banging the bowl around if the requested service is not forthcoming quickly enough. I had set up a timer to alert me when the time to watch the NBC evening news has come. The dog is right behind me when I venture into the kitchen, and he supervises the refill operation. He stares at me as I shovel food into the bowl; I learned to interpret that as the signal for "more." I pour myself a glass of Perrier, in compliance with my committed effort to slow my alcohol intake. I had promised myself that the frequent trips to recycle empty bottles will from now on occur at slightly longer intervals.

Not much going on the local news, but it gets a little livelier at the national level. The Los Alamos fire update comes after the first commercial, no longer being hot news. Lacking new developments or interview footage, the public interest is waning. All knowledgeable participants and observers are either dead, in prison, or like me, close-mouthed under threat of penalty of imprisonment.

I would have missed it when an SMS arrived, had the phone not made a gentle one-eighth clockwise turn on the desk when the vibrating buzzer did its job. I lean over to discern the sender's name or number, or even the subject line. Unknown number, 416 area code, no subject line. A robocall most likely, since I don't have many friends left in Toronto.

Then I see the message. "Feeling like dinner?" Not a robocall. I wait. "Where you fell in love with Chile en Nogada?" I fall in love about twice a day, so that does not narrow it down by much. While I am getting an inkling, I dare not really hope who this might be. If it is, she has one hell of a memory. The fact that it's a message with no sender name, gives me a shiver. My fingers fly over the phone. "My place?" Seconds later, "Further south!" Now I remember talking about my fascination with Mexican food, not all that long ago. Further south, she said. Mexico. "When?" is the obvious next question. "Tuesday. Six Ish." Can do. Better make sure we are on the same page. "My phone will be off. Turn yours off as well. Walk to the restaurant. As in Famous Latin Lover." She will get it. Don Juan; I remember telling her the name of the place, way back when I desperately tried to bring up anything sexual or at least suggestive in the conversation.

American flies from Albuquerque non-stop to Puerto Vallarta. Twice daily. Now the question is: Who's watching me, my cell, and my credit cards? Probably not the rest of the Crooks, that show is essentially over. Not the Feds—that show is over as well. The paparazzi? Not likely. Ronan Farrow? Or a clone thereof? The story is not worth writing a book about, not yet. I am not in any trouble, or of any interest to virtually anyone, other than the leasing company. And they are not likely to tap my phone or follow me to Mexico.

It turns out I have enough miles to fly on a freebie economy, last row, a non-reclining seat on the 7:45 AM out of Albuquerque. And frequent flyer ticket travel leaves no credit card record; I still had some credit from a cancelled flight to pay for the tax. In Mexico, cabs take cash. I plan to leave no trail.

Flying commercially ceased to be the thrill it once was.

The arrival hall in Puerto Vallarta is always a zoo. After elbowing through the crowd of confused or lost tourists and waving away the usual sharp-eyed hawkers who offer free meals in exchange for a high-pressure sales pitch for a timeshare contract, I step into the sweltering heat. In case one thinks that the situation outside Customs will calm down, one is mistaken. It gets worse as the day goes by, so an early incoming flight is a good thing. I have never figured out the logic behind the system (and, while invisible to the naked eye, a system MUST exist) of how one finds one's shuttle bus, limo or taxi at Puerto Vallarta airport. Some magic process that involves ambiguous directions and much finger-pointing initiates the hunt. Right about when I am willing to give up and go back for more punishment, I find my pre-arranged cab. He says his name is Jesus. His mother must have had high hopes for him at one time, and she might by now be disappointed by the achievements of her offspring. No bragging rights? He is delighted to learn that, A., I speak some Spanish, B., I know where I am going, and C., I will offer cash in dollars. Lest I forget: D., no receipt required. We are becoming friends real fast.

We are heading north towards Tepic on interstate 200. About half an hour north of the airport, a left turn at a gas station takes us to Sayulita. This sweet little ex-fishing village has turned into a cute resort town, mostly frequented by those who have nothing but disdain for the gringo crowds that haunt Puerto Vallarta. Sayulita means lots of surfers. The rednecks stay in the big chain hotels back in Vallarta, eat at Senor Frogs, and shop at the Malecon. A much more sophisticated tourist ventures here, where the food is better, cheaper, and—Allah Be Praised— mostly devoid of mac and cheese. That should keep the mob away.

I am early enough to hunt for a place to stay. At the central plaza where Jesus drops me off, right at the corner, is a real estate broker. All offers on display in the window are in dollars, so Mexicans have to convert the number to pesos. That tells me something about the prospect base. I figure that half of the gringos who own condos here rent them out between visits. A gleaming set of oversized teeth (think Sophia Loren) greets me warmly. I divulge that I am looking for a charming, quiet place to stay for a few days, moving in right now. I am willing to prepay, again, cash, dollars, no receipt required (magic words in a country with a dysfunctional tax collection system). I am told that a Susan with no last name will be waiting for me in half an hour, the location provided on a sliver of torn off paper realistically too small for the address.

On the main drag is a pizzeria I fondly remember from a visit years ago. No one there remembers me. I, however, remember that the Margarita con Chile was a revelation. It is no longer on the menu, so I settle for a beer.

Susan turns out to be in her fifties, from Kalamazoo, charming and well dressed. I must re-evaluate my sinister expectations regarding fashion shopping in Kalamazoo. The room turns out to be a full apartment with a separate bedroom but lacking a full kitchen. I am not planning to do much cooking. The king size bed, on the other hand, might turn out to be useful. From the apartment, it's a touch too far to walk to the restaurant to meet my date, but Susan from Kalamazoo is heading into town and gives me a ride back to the plaza.

It is almost five-thirty when I start heading on foot towards Don Juan, a lovely little restaurant off the beaten path in the direction of Punta de Mita. As I walk in, it's just about six, the smells hit me, and I am overwhelmed with memories of meals, years earlier, devoured at this very spot.

At six, the place is still mostly empty. A family, spanning four generations, the oldest on a walker, the youngest in diapers, are getting up, ready to leave. A head, male, bald and sweaty, appears and is quickly retracted from the tiny kitchen. A few seconds later, a female head re-appears. Moments later, her body follows. I remember them as the chef owner and his wife from years ago. She seems to have an inkling that I had been here before but can't place me.

To get the show on the road, I solicit "Un Cerveza por favor." Her English has improved considerably since my last meal, and she responds in acceptable English with "Woood you like una Corona? Pacifico? Tecate? Negra Modelo? Bohemia?" I stick with Pacifico. She continues with a well-rehearsed "Wiiill you be comer, I mean dining alone tonight?" I hesitate. If Erin does not show, I will look stood up, and that is not acceptable. A man has his pride. Yet, why am I concerned with what image I project? "No, I am planning to have dinner with a friend." The two extra place sets and cutlery are swept up in an instant. Two sets of neatly printed menus arrive at the same time the beer shows up. The unsolicited ice-cold glass demonstrates what a few great reviews on TripAdvisor will do to an eatery's pride.

The time is just past six by now. Through the open door, I notice a car driving by slowly and turning around to park and unload in front of the entrance. Is this a low pass to see if I am here and by myself before committing?

If I had not been expecting her, I would have sat at the table next to her without recognizing her. A reasonable assumption is that the full head of curly hair is a wig. The round, cobalt-blue tinted steampunk style glasses go well with the lack of makeup and the gray cargo pants: a hoodie and a small backpack complete the setup. From working on movie sets, I am aware of how difficult it can be to turn a swan into an ugly duckling. Though that is easier than the other way around, she had done an admirable job. The packaging indicates a desire to be ignored and categorized as yet another anonymous dated hippy. I am waiting for some facial expression that reveals what is coming my way. Soon I recognize the lowered eyes and the guilty demeanor we all know from pets who done wrong. Like getting caught eating a sofa.

I had given much thought as to how I should deal with an eventual encounter long before the text message that lured me here. Among the reactions designed for a difficult to predict scene, I had prepared some wisecracks rather than chastisement. Nothing, however, had prepared me for what was now standing next to my table. I stand up slowly, squeeze Erin's hand, and pull out her chair. A mildly cynical "Thanks for skipping the false mustache" whispered under my breath is the best I can come up with on short notice. We skip the hug, and I do my best to project an image of two people who meet to discuss sharing a car to somewhere else. The scene in *Casablanca*, where Humphrey Bogart meets Ingrid Bergman again, flashes before my eyes.

"So, how have you been?" does not do a lot of justice to what we have shared in the past. My words, not hers. Seconds pass. "I can recommend Chile en Nogada. The 2015 Pacifico is not bad either." I see a hint of moistness form in her eyes. Glad to see that this is difficult for her as well. Since she shows up sans helicopter, yet with no visible bandages, I breathe a sigh of relief. "Where did you park?" She is, at the same time, sorry to have abandoned me, yet proud of the fact that she horsed a helicopter into the air and is now here to talk about it.

I was afraid of what comes next. "Out of gas. On an abandoned Airpark near Columbus, New Mexico. Hacienda somethingoranother."

"I know where that is. It's an airport just north of the border. The FAA's designation is NM78. Where in

1916 Pancho Villa came across the border on a raid. So, it's not a loss." Why there?

Erin needs to confess that she was heading for Puerto Palomas de Villa on the Mexican side when the low fuel light came on. I feel less stupid now because I had my Bell Long Ranger cleaned right before she took off with it. I also since had spent hours bringing the Logbooks up to date, ready for the NTSB just in case it was, despite generally accepted low expectations, found.

"Did you bend it? You got hurt?"

She waves her hand in a "…. not bent, stepped into some thorns, got dusty, that's all" message." The money? I am not interested in sharing the money. I am interested in her getting away with it. She says "Gone" and at the same time, her hand instinctively moves towards her backpack. Not gone, is it?

I need to probe a little here; her confession is coming across as hesitant. Since I just learned that my aircraft still exists, I lust to hear the gory details, to learn of the plan.

I burst out "Why there? Did you go west on the Mexico side or through Arizona? Why Sayulita?" and she responds with "later."

Maria, or whatever her name is, shows up the second time to take orders. Other guests have shown up as well, so the message is to get cracking. We haven't even glanced at the menu. Since we are here to meet and deal with our past (and possibly our future), food is of secondary importance, and Erin does not even try to fake any interest. Sometimes kicking a stuck conversation back on track is the man's job. I know her tastes. I know her style. I know her. I want her.

Maria's notepad comes out, and I start: "We will share a Ceviche as the first course. Bring the lady a Pacifico. We will both have the Chile en Nogada. For nostalgic reasons." Maria can't figure out what that means. She nods, grabs the menus, and buzzes off to inform the Jefe. Now I see a tear roll down Erin's cheek. Harry, will you please cut back on the drama?

"I am so sorry." Confusion must by now have reached my face.

"What for?" I inquire.

"The betrayal." I understand. I bet she would have felt that way even without the wild night. Perhaps, even this late in the game, it might be possible to make this plural—as in nights?

"You wanted to see me?" Her eyes tell me that she missed me. I am trying very hard not to return the sentiment—no need to increase the agony.

"Look, this. . . " I get stuck. Pause. "Look, this is going nowhere. Us is going nowhere. At least for now. You have no life left up north – too many people wondering about you, looking for you. The Feds consider the contents of that suitcase theirs and theirs alone. Wondering how much of the loot went with you. Stay south of the border. Being seen with you makes me look guilty of something. Not sure what, beyond poor judgment. Puts me at risk. On that topic: Have you been careful? Looked behind you about being followed? You clean?" She does not know much about Ian's demise. Neither does she know about the showdown in Divisadero.

"I am clean." I'll check when we leave. Three tables are occupied by now. The guests that have arrived since we got here are unlikely shadows.

Her beer and our Ceviche arrive. We both drink our beer. She sips hers. I suck mine down until it is almost gone. The waitress takes note; the always reliable circular motion finger signaling "more beer" is acknowledged. Initially, no one touches the Ceviche; at some point, it is me who grabs a small fork, and I nibble just a bit short of enthusiastic since otherwise, the word will get back to the kitchen to hold back the main course.

The mood is somber, sort of depressed. Finally, she decides that Ceviche is healthy after all and takes a timid, lust-less bite herself. More guests show up and sit on tables too close for our privacy. We move to another table in a corner under an umbrella that is not providing much shade but traps the stifling heat. I sit facing the room and have her facing toward me and the outside wall. By now, I am pretty much a bundle of paranoia, more on her behalf than mine. Competent shadows can and will lip-read. At least now, we are relatively safe from accidentally being overheard.

I inquire, "So, where did you arrive from?" and at first, I get no response. After a few seconds, a sad smile precedes what I recognize as a scene from an old Western with Yul Brynner, when he was asked the same question and he responded with a wordless thumb pointing back over his shoulder. I ask, "Where are you heading now?" next, just like Jules did, and I get the expected silent thumb pointing ahead. The name of the movie comes back to me just in time. *The Magnificent Seven,* in my humble opinion, a masterpiece.

While the uninformative answer to the first question does not bother me, being of historical value only, her reluctance to say where she is going next does. "Why did you send the SMS suggesting for us to meet?"

Maybe she hadn't asked herself the hard Why? I did not expect her reply to be, "To see if you would show up." Our ability to engage in scintillating small talk has come to an early end. "I needed to see you again." Her words, my feelings.

Maria shows up with the main course; she admonishes us with a stern look for not having devoured the Ceviche and takes off with most of it. By New Mexican standards, the Ceviche had been a touch too wimpy, so just before Maria grabbed our first course, I do manage to hang on to the salsa and the hot sauce in case it is going to be needed later. I am here to see the lust of my life, why the hell am I worried if the food isn't spicy enough? Because my life isn't spicy enough. At least there was no kale in it.

I persist, repeating, "Where are you heading?" I need to know for practical reasons: regardless of where she is heading, I will head in the opposite direction. That is not what I want to do; that is what I must do. What I want to do is take her on a cruise through the Caribbean until all her money is gone, since cruises are not watched with the same determination as planes, cars and border crossings by the Feds who know that some of that fine cash might be in her backpack.

My next question is, "Do you have everything you need?" I am thinking of passports, prepaid credit cards, a change of clothes for more elegant occasions than this one. She nods. I say, "If you don't feel comfortable talking about it, I am not offended. I understand the concept of risk management, and I realize that everything and everyone in your past is now considered a risk."

She puts down her fork, looks at me with smoky eyes, and says, "I have a passport, some money, and a ticket on the TicaBus all the way to Panama City. To screw with anyone trying to track me down, I will get off the bus in Costa Rica—probably in Tamarindo. That place is firmly in the hand of the gringo surfers. I should be able to blend in."

"And then?" I inquire. She tells me to wait for a text message. Not unreasonable since it worked the first time. We munch away in silence. It's eerily quiet, and the piped-in music is on a low volume with neither of us daring to say "Play it again, Sam." All I can hope is that her story ends better than Selma and Louise.

She looks at me and says, "Yours is better."

"What?" and I figure out what she meant just in time. She was talking about the main course. Yet neither of us has finished the meal. I will not be greeted at Don Juan with the same warmth next time. The server shows up and wants to know, "Wanna coffee? Flan?" Neither of us does.

I go to the bathroom, and when I get back, she is gone.

I guess we will always have Santa Fe.

About the Author

Engineer. Gourmand. Corporate executive. Entrepreneur. Fixed- and rotary-wing commercial pilot. Raconteur. Keynote speaker. Architect. Polyglot. Philanthropist.

Author.

These are just some of the words used to describe Manfred Leuthard, the author of the new seat-of-your-pants thriller *Broken Arrow: A Nuke Goes Missing*, available through Amazon and many other bookstores.

Leuthard has seen and done it all—or at least a whole bunch of it. He can make a paella that's out of this world. Or cross the country in a gyroplane he built, sharing pilot duties with his wife and licensed pilot Lilo. As a way of transitioning out of the corporate snake pit, Manfred bought a helicopter and started his own helicopter service. His clients were tourists, utility companies, ranchers and the movie industry. (That's him, behind the stick on *Wild Hogs, 3:10 to Yuma* and many other hit movies.)

This background—diverse, international, complex—and his extraordinary ability to grasp and articulate the details of technology come together in his first novel, written over a two-year period, with many of hours of research to get every detail just right. From the grittiest face-to-face battles between the men intent on selling nuclear weaponry to the highest bidder and the men intent on stopping them, to the quietest moments of passion and love, Leuthard unravels a heart-pounding story you won't—no, you *won't be able to*—put down. After having lived all over the world—he's an American and Swiss citizen—today Manfred and Lilo are now nestled in the tight-knit community of Santa Fe, New Mexico. In fact, that just might be him at the café, weaving another entrancing tale for his friends.

Made in the USA
Middletown, DE
20 February 2022

61536246R00189